Noongar
Bush
Tucker

The Charles and Joy Staples South West Region Publications Fund was established in 1984 on the basis of a generous donation to The University of Western Australia by Charles and Joy Staples.

The purpose of the Fund is to highlight all aspects of the South West region of Western Australia, a geographical area much loved by Charles and Joy Staples, so as to assist the people of the South West region and those in government and private organisations concerned with South West projects to appreciate the needs and possibilities of the region in the widest possible historical perspective.

The fund is administered by a committee whose aims are to make possible the publication by UWA Publishing of research and writing in any discipline relevant to the South West region.

Charles and Joy Staples South West Region Publications Fund titles

1987
A Tribute to the Group Settlers
Philip E. M. Blond

1992
For Their Own Good: Aborigines and Government in the Southwest of Western Australia, 1900–1940
Anna Haebich

1993
Portraits of the South West
B. K. de Garis

A Guide to Sources for the History of South Western Australia
Compiled by Ronald Richards

1994
Jardee: The Mill That Cheated Time
Doreen Owens

1995
Dearest Isabella: Life and Letters of Isabella Ferguson, 1819–1910
Prue Joske

Blacklegs: The Scottish Colliery Strike of 1911 Bill Latter

1997
Barefoot in the Creek: A Group Settlement Childhood in Margaret River L. C. Burton

Ritualist on a Tricycle: Frederick Goldsmith, Church, Nationalism and Society in Western Australia
Colin Holden

Western Australia as it is Today, 1906
Leopoldo Zunini, Royal Consul of Italy, edited and translated by Richard Bosworth and Margot Melia

2002
The South West from Dawn till Dusk
Rob Olver

2003
Contested Country: A History of the Northcliffe Area, Western Australia
Patricia Crawford and Ian Crawford

2004
Orchard and Mill: The Story of Bill Lee, South-West Pioneer
Lyn Adams

2005
Richard Spencer: Napoleonic War Naval Hero and Australian Pioneer
Gwen Chessell

2006
A Story to Tell (reprinted 2012)
Laurel Nannup

2008
Alexander Collie: Colonial Surgeon, Naturalist and Explorer
Gwen Chessell

The Zealous Conservator: A Life of Charles Lane Poole
John Dargavel

2009
"It's Still in My Heart, This is My Country": The Single Noongar Claim History
South West Aboriginal Land and Sea Council, John Host with Chris Owen

Shaking Hands on the Fringe: Negotiating the Aboriginal World at King George's Sound
Tiffany Shellam

2011
Noongar Mambara Bakitj and Mamang
Kim Scott and Wirlomin Noongar Language and Stories Project

Guy Grey-Smith: Life Force
Andrew Gaynor

2013
Dwoort Baal Kaat and Yira Boornak Nyininy
Kim Scott and Wirlomin Noongar Language and Stories Project

2014
A Boy's Short Life: The Story of Warren Braedon/Louis Johnson
Anna Haebich and Steve Mickler

Plant Life on the Sandplains: A Global Biodiversity Hotspot
Hans Lambers

Fire and Hearth (revised facsimile edition)
Sylvia Hallam

2015
Running Out? Water in Western Australia
Ruth Morgan

A Journey Travelled: Aboriginal–European Relations at Albany and Surrounding Regions from First Colonial Contact to 1926
Murray Arnold

The Southwest: Australia's Biodiversity Hotspot
Victoria Laurie

Invisible Country: South-West Australia: Understanding a Landscape
Bill Bunbury

2016
Noongar Bush Medicine: Medicinal Plants of the South-West of Western Australia
Vivienne Hansen and John Horsfall

2017
Never Again: Reflections on Environmental Responsibility After Roe 8
Edited by Andrea Gaynor, Peter Newman and Philip Jennings

Ngaawily Nop and Noorn
Kim Scott and Wirlomin Noongar Language and Stories Project

2018
Dancing in Shadows: Histories of Nyungar Performance
Anna Haebich

Noongar
Bush
Tucker

BUSH FOOD PLANTS AND FUNGI OF THE SOUTH-WEST OF WESTERN AUSTRALIA

VIVIENNE HANSEN AND
JOHN HORSFALL

U W
A P
UWA PUBLISHING

First published in 2019 by
UWA Publishing
Crawley, Western Australia 6009
www.uwap.uwa.edu.au
UWAP is an imprint of UWA Publishing
a division of The University of Western Australia

**THE UNIVERSITY OF
WESTERN
AUSTRALIA**

ISBN: 978-1-76080-042-0 (paperback)

Design by Upside Creative

Front cover photo: Candle Cranberry, *Astroloma ciliatum*,
photographer Jean Hort

Back cover photos: (top) Branched Catspaw, *Anigozanthos onycis*,
photographer unknown

(bottom left) Common Nardoo, *Marsilea drummondii*,
photographer John Horsfall

(bottom right) Albany Bottlebrush, *Callistemon glaucus*,
photographer unknown

Printed by McPherson's Printing Group

uwapublishing

Foreword

The end result for the people that read this book will be the expansion of knowledge about a group of people that are now recognised as belonging to the longest continuous, unbroken culture on Earth. Today these people are known as the Noongar people and they occupy the south-west of Western Australia. This region is known as one of the Earth's biodiversity hot spots.

It provided the people a wide range of natural food resources, all jam-packed full of the essentials needed to sustain human life. While this region provided its ancient people with birds, animals, fish and reptiles as food, this book is about the abundance of plant material that was eaten. Botanists estimate there are in excess of 10,000 species of plants in Noongar country and what most Australian people do not know is that Noongar people harvested all their food according to a deep spiritual food law. This food law was connected to a six-season cycle of movement across Noongar land; each season had its own basic diet. It was also inextricably linked to a social order with a rigidly enforced marriage law. This combined with the belief that you could only eat food resources in accordance with your kinship, which was determined by the marriage law.

The Noongar world view is, 'the spiritual world actions the physical world'. This book gives a large sample of some of the many plants that provided sustenance for Noongar people over many thousands of years. Without doubt one of the most important aspects of this book is it leaves a legacy about a sample of bush foods used in the south-west of Western Australia for future generations. My greatest hope is that young Nyoongar people will embrace this knowledge and build upon it. Congratulations to all who have contributed.

Dr Noel Nannup
Noongar Elder, storyteller and cultural guide

Contents

DISCLAIMER

This book has been written based on information accumulated by the authors from personal knowledge passed on from family members, third parties (including websites, records, documents that other parties have prepared), as well as from Aboriginal Elders with traditional bush tucker knowledge. While the authors have used their best endeavours to produce an accurate account of plants and fungi used as a food source by the Noongar people of the south-west of Western Australia, they do not warrant or make any claim as to the accuracy or otherwise of the information contained in the work and accept no responsibility whatsoever in the event of any inaccurate information contained in the book. It is the authors' recommendation that people wishing to use the plants and fungi described in this book for culinary purposes for themselves, family or friends, consult with Elders and traditional bush tucker gatherers who have knowledge of the plants and fungi in their area before consuming parts of such plants and fungi. People also need to familiarise themselves with the Western Australian laws relating to the flora of the south-west. All native plants on Crown land are protected in Western Australia by law. Section 171 of the *Biodiversity Conservation Act 2016* states that you need a licence to take part or all of any native plant on Crown land, or permission from the owners if the flora is on privately owned land. In Western Australia the penalties are quite severe if people disregard the law related to flora and fauna.

Section 182 of the *Biodiversity Conservation Act 2016* implies that people of Aboriginal descent may take flora and fauna for customary purposes, that is for ceremonial, food or medicinal purposes, providing that they comply with the parts of the Act that relate to the taking of flora. Aboriginal persons are advised to read Section 182 of the Act relating to Aboriginal people. A copy of the Act can be viewed online at:

www5.austlii.edu.au/au/legis/wa/num_act/bca201624o2016355/

A licence is also needed to collect fungi on Crown land in Western Australia. People collecting wild fungi to eat need to check with a fungi expert before eating wild mushrooms as there are poisonous look-alikes that can cause death if eaten.

Introduction

For over 200 years non-Aboriginal Australians have been led to believe, through primary and secondary school curriculums, that Aboriginal Australians, before colonisation, were nomadic hunters and gatherers who lived in temporary shelters. Evidence has recently come to light, gleened from the journals of early explorers and settlers, that this was far from the truth. In fact, in some areas of Australia, evidence has been uncovered that Aboriginal communities lived in permanent or semi-permanent settlements and engaged in extensive agriculture and aquaculture (Pascoe, 2014). There is also evidence of this in the journals of prominent Western Australian explorers and settlers.

Sir George Grey (1841), an early explorer of Western Australia, on his trek from Gantheaume Bay to the Hutt River, wrote in his journal:

> We now crossed the dry bed of a stream and from that emerged upon a tract of light fertile soil, quite overrun with warran plants, the root of which is a favourite article of food with the natives. This was the first time we had yet seen this plant on our journey, and now for three and a half consecutive miles we traversed a fertile piece of land literally perforated with the holes the natives had made to dig this root; indeed, we could with difficulty walk across it on that account, whilst this tract extended east and west as far as we could see.

> It was now evident that we had entered the most thickly-populated district of Australia that I had yet observed, and moreover one which must have been inhabited for a long series of years, for more had here been done to secure a provision from the ground by hard manual labour than I could have believed it in the power of uncivilised man to accomplish. After crossing

a low limestone range, we came down upon another equally fertile warran ground, bounded eastward by a high range of rocky limestone hills, luxuriantly grassed, and westward by a low range of similar formation.

There is also some evidence of sophisticated methods of aquaculture in Australia before colonisation. The Gunditjmara people in the Lake Condah region of western Victoria were eel farmers. To breed eels, they modified more than 100 square kilometres of the landscape by constructing artificial ponds across the grassy wetlands and digging channels to connect them. The whole scheme was systematically punctuated with eel traps (Phillips, 2003).

George Moore (1884b), a prominent Western Australian explorer, speaking of his trek up the Kalgan River that runs into Oyster Harbour on the south coast of Western Australia, wrote in his diary:

We walked higher up the river, which was here a running stream about twenty-five yards broad, crossed in several places by ledges of rock, where the natives had constructed ingenious weirs for taking fish, which appeared to be abundant.

Remains of fish traps made from brushwood have been found on the Serpentine and the Murray rivers in the south-west of Western Australia (Dix and Meagher, 1976).

In Brewarrina, northern New South Wales, there is evidence that Aboriginal Australians have been involved in aquaculture for over 40,000 years. The sophisticated fish traps there, known in the local Aboriginal language as Baiame's Ngunnhuare, on a tributary of the Barwon River, are an elaborate network of rock weirs and pools that stretch for half a kilometre along the riverbed. They can still be seen today.

Kalgan River fish traps

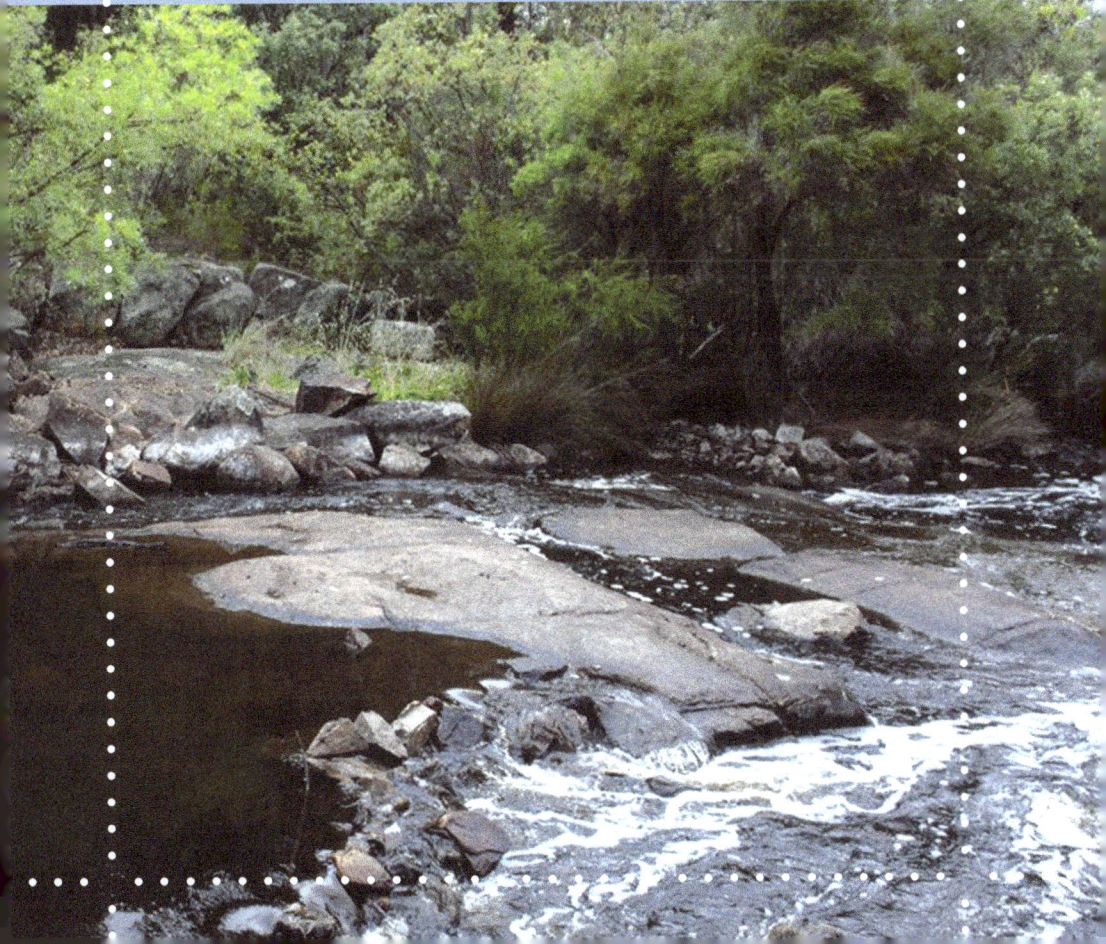

Evidence has also come to light that, in some areas of Australia, Aboriginal Australians built permanent and semi-permanent dwellings that were quite elaborate before settlement by Europeans. For example, Pascoe (2014), after extensive research that included scouring the journals of Charles Sturt, another prominent Australian explorer, wrote:

> Sturt saw buildings in a number of different locations, including several at Strzelecki Creek in 1845, and he made sketches of many. The entrance of one was 14.5 metres wide and two metres high, the roof having been plastered with a thick coating of clay.
>
> In another area he saw huts made with strong elliptical arches, covered with boughs and rendered with a thick coating of clay so that the huts were impervious to wind and heat.

Archeologists working on Rosemary Island in the Dampier Archipelago off Australia's north-west coast have found evidence of stone houses dating back 9,000 years. They have found circular stone foundations on the island and believe that the island was connected to the mainland up to 8,000 years ago (Wahlquist, 2016).

There are many other descriptions in Bruce Pascoe's (2014) book *Dark Emu, Black Seeds: Agriculture or Accident?* of permanent and semi-permanent dwellings that preceeded colonisation, including stone houses in Victoria, evidence of which has almost been obliterated by settlers that took over the land and cleared it for farming. He also produced evidence of the cultivation and storage of grain.

Brough Smythe (1840) cited in Williams (1984) wrote of some permanent Aboriginal dwellings in Victoria:

Blacks, about 50 miles N.E. of Port Fairy, by what is termed the Scrubby Creek, before settlers came among them had a regular Village. My informant who drew this states that there were between 20–30 evidently some of them big enough to hold a dozen people, their shape as under an aperture at top to let out smoke, which in rainy weather they covered with large sod, The form like a Bee Hive about 6 feet high + or – and about 10 feet in diameter. An opening about 3 feet for a door way which they could close at night with piece of bark.

Noongars of the Bibbulmun Nation

For those readers who haven't read our first book *Noongar Bush Medicine: Medicinal Plants of the South-West of Western Australia (2016),* we shall give a brief account of Noongar history and culture.

Recent genetic marker studies have revealed that the Noongar people of the south-west of Western Australia have inhabited this area of Australia for over 45,000 years (Bradshaw Foundation, 2011). The land or 'country' of our Noongar people stretches from Geraldton to Esperance, comprising an area of land of approximately 3 million hectares with a coastline that covers 16,000 kilometres. Noongar people had their own language, laws and customs and gathered regularly for celebrations, trade, marriage arrangements and other purposes. They lived well in their country with a varied diet depending on the seasons and location.

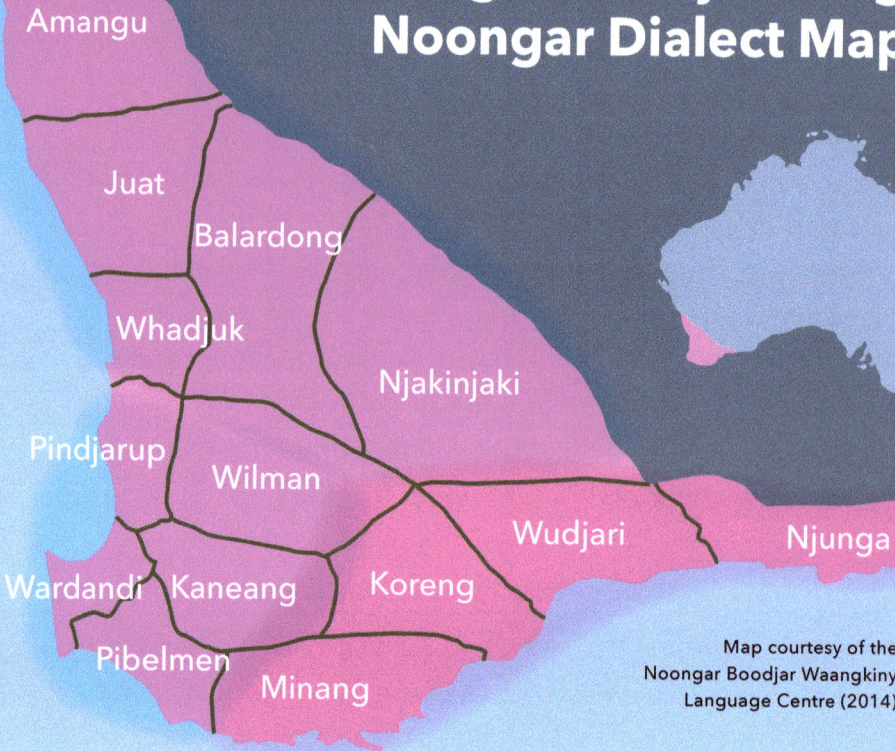

Noongar Boodja Wongki
Noongar Dialect Map

Amangu

Juat

Balardong

Whadjuk

Njakinjaki

Pindjarup

Wilman

Wudjari

Njunga

Wardandi   Kaneang   Koreng

Pibelmen

Minang

Map courtesy of the
Noongar Boodjar Waangkiny
Language Centre (2014)

According to Tindale (1974), Noongar country is occupied by fourteen different dialect groups. He identified them as being Amangu, Ballardong, Yued, Kaneang, Koreng, Mineng, Njakinjaki, Njunga, Pibelmen, Binjareb, Wardandi, Whadjuk, Wilman and Wudjari as per the above map based on Tindale's findings. Noongar people traditionally spoke dialects of the Noongar language, a member of the large Pama-Nyungan language family.

The Pama-Nyungan languages are the most widespread family of Aboriginal Australian languages, containing perhaps 300 languages. The name 'Pama-Nyungan' is derived from the names of the two most widely separated groups, the Pama languages of the north-east and the Nyungan languages of the south-west. The words *pama* and *nyunga* mean 'man' in their respective languages (Frawley, 2004).

The spelling 'Noongar' was supported by Great Southern people at a meeting in Narrogin in 1992 and remains in common use on the south coast and Great Southern regions of Western Australia. Other ways of spelling Noongar that have been used include Nyungar, Nyoongar, Nyoongah, Nyungah, Nyugah, Yungar and Noonga (Noongar Boodjar Waangkiny Language Centre, 2014).

Noongars enjoyed a diverse diet and had an intimate knowledge of edible plants and when and where they could be found. Some of these plants were potentially poisonous, but Noongar people knew what to do to make them edible. Flowers from the Wattle, Eucalypt, Banksia, Grevillea and Melaleuca trees provided nectar that was either sucked directly from the flower or soaked in water to make a sweet drink called mungitch or neip.

Trees provided the materials necessary for the making of implements from spears, boomerangs, digging sticks and bowls. Bark (*boort*) provided shelter and was also used to wrap food for cooking. Gum from the Balga was used in making stone implements that were used for a variety of purposes. The stone was quarried from a wide area. Grinding stones, spears, quartz rocks, ochres and clays were very popular trading items for Noongars.

Bark shelters were built in the cold winters and the Noongars wore kangaroo skin cloaks (booka) for warmth. The cloaks were made from the skins of the kangaroo, which they pegged out on the ground to dry. The skins were then cut with a stone knife into the desired shape and the inner surface was scraped until the skin became very soft and pliable. Once this was completed the skins were then sewn together with animal sinews and rubbed with grease and red ochre.

Firesticks were carried when travelling long distances from the camps (kullarks). These firesticks were used to start a fire and to keep warm in the cold. When it rained the firesticks were usually carried under their cloaks.

There are six seasons for Noongars and their diet was based on the seasons. They knew when the seasons changed by the weather patterns, the movement of the stars, the behaviour of the birds and the lifecycle of plants. Kangaroos, ducks and fish were abundant as were turtle, fish, marron, emus, turkey, wallaby, snakes and lizards. Fish traps were used to catch fish and firestick farming was practised, improving the grass and to drive out small game. Noongar law required that no seed-bearing plants could be dug up until after flowering. Noongars only took what they needed. All food that was brought back to camp from hunting and foraging was shared amongst the group, so nobody went hungry.

The six-season calendar outlined below is extremely important to all Noongar people, as it is a guide to what nature is doing at every stage of the year, as well as helping them understand respect for the land in relation to plant and animal fertility cycles and land and animal preservation.

For many Noongars colonisation changed their diet dramatically. As settlers cleared land for crop farming and raising sheep and cattle, Noongars gained less and less access to their traditional hunting grounds and came to rely more and more on rations of tea, sugar and flour, and of course meagre, often insuffient, mission food, such as porridge and watery stews, for those confined to missions. Some were able to supplement their diet with rabbits and bush food.

The Noongar Seasons

Noongar Season (Bonar)	Months	Weather	Noongar Activities
Birak or Beruc	December and January	Hot and dry	Becoming hotter. Noongars burned sections of scrubland to force animals into the open. The Christmas Tree is in bloom. Mullet and bream are plentiful. Mungitch, a drink made from nectar, was made from Banksias and Bottlebrushes.
Bunuru or Meertilluc	February and March	Warm easterly winds	Hottest part of the year, with sparse rainfall throughout. Noongar moved to estuaries for fishing. This is the start of the salmon and herring season. Karda (goanna) eggs are plentiful.
Djeran, Wanyarang or Pourner	April and May	Cool and pleasant	Cooler weather begins. Fishing continued and bulbs, such as the root bulbs of Yanget (Bullrushes), and seeds were collected for food. This was a good time to hunt for waitj (emu), freshwater fish, frogs and turtles. Numbit (Marri) blossoms were sucked for their nectar.
Makuru Mawkur or Maggoro	June and July	Cold and wet	Cold fronts continue. This is usually the wettest part of the year. The rains replenish inland water resources. Wild Carrot and Native Potatoes are ready to harvest. Malting swans (mali) became easy prey. Kangaroo (yonga), bandicoot (quenda) and possums (kumal) were hunted.

Noongar Season (Bonar)	Months	Weather	Noongar Activities
Djilba or Meerningal	August and September	Cold with lessening rains	Usually the coldest part of the year, with clear, cold days and nights, and warmer, rainy and windy periods. Roots (bwoor) were harvested and emus, possums and kangaroo were still hunted. Eggs were plentiful.
Kambarang or Maungernan	October and November	Warming, rains finishing	Longer dry periods and fewer cold fronts cross the coast. This is the height of the wildflower season and the flowers are full of nectar. The Noongar moved towards the coast where frogs, tortoises and freshwater crayfish were caught.

Adapted from Rainbow Coast (2017) and Denmark Arts (2005)

This book is an attempt by the authors to gather, record and publish information on plants and fungi used by the Noongars of the south-west of Western Australia for food before colonisation; and in so doing it ensures that the traditional knowledge is not lost forever with the passing of Elders.

As this book goes to press, Aboriginal and Torres Strait Islander Australians on average are still dying years earlier than non-Aboriginal Australians. They are also suffering higher rates of cardiovascular disease, type 2 diabetes, cancer, chronic lung diseases, and end-stage renal disease. It is hoped that this book may encourage Aboriginal and Torres Strait Islanders to bypass fast-food outlets and processed food and drinks high in sugar, salt and fats and look at a more traditional diet of lean meats, whole grains, root vegetables, green vegetables, fruits and more traditional beverages with less sugar.

About the Authors

For those readers who have not read our first book, *Noongar Bush Medicine: Medicinal Plants of the South-West of Western Australia*, here are our stories again.

Vivienne's Story

I am a Balladong Wadjuk Yorga from the Bibbulmun Nation or Noongar people of the south-west of Western Australia. I was born in Beverley and my childhood was spent in Brookton and the surrounding regions of Noongar country. My mother was Myrtle, who was the youngest child of Kate Collard and Norman Bennell, and it was they who raised me until my grandmother died. After the death of my grandmother I went to live with my mother's sister, Aunty Olive, and her husband, Uncle Clarrie McGuire. These family members and older uncles, aunts and cousins raised me to have a strong sense of respect, appreciation and knowledge of Noongar identity, culture and language. Like all my relatives, this close connection to country enabled me to explore the local bushlands and develop a deep understanding and knowledge of traditional bush tucker, bush medicine, remedies and practices.

Grandfather was a healer like his father before him, and he and his two brothers, Granny Felix and Granny Bert, told us stories about our Noongar people and culture. They taught us how to look for signs in our surrounds such as the abundance of the blossoms on the gum trees, which could tell us about the coming seasons and weather patterns. My Grandfather Norman and his brothers taught us about other signs and how to hunt for possum and goanna. We were also taught how to perform certain cultural ceremonies when we are near water or places of special significance. This was to acknowledge the land, our Mother Earth, for all she provides for our people.

Vivienne Hansen

My aunties and older cousins took us walking through the bush where we gathered the berries and yams, collected gum and sucked the sweet nectar from the flowers of certain trees and plants when they were in season.

Even today, the seasons play a vital role in medicine as some plants are only available after a rainy season or need fire to regrow. We were taught to only collect what we need at that particular time; there was no need to cut an entire tree down when we only required a handful of leaves. I also learned that it was very important not to trespass on another group's area without their permission.

After Nanna Kate's death, life with my aunt and uncle continued along these same ways but we got to go out in the bush more regularly as Uncle Clarrie worked on a lot of farms around Brookton. At this time in my life, many of the farms had an abundance of bushland, as much of the land had not been cleared for crops. One of the farms we lived on was right next door to the state forest between Brookton and Kelmscott. Our time there gave me many opportunities to explore the bush and plants that grew there and I was always asking Uncle and Aunt what they were used for. I did not always get answers to all my questions but that is when my interest in native plants began to grow and the foundations were laid for my work in this area today.

In 2008 I undertook formal training at the Marr Moorditj Foundation and completed Certificate IV in Bush and Western Herbal Medicine. I am very proud to be the first Indigenous member of the National Herbalist Association of Australia and a presenter at the 7th International Conference on Herbal Medicine 2012 in Coolangatta, Queensland.

Whilst enrolled at Marr Moorditj, I became aware that much of the information published on Aboriginal bush medicine did not contain a great deal of information on Noongar medicines and that the majority of the works published were by non-Aboriginal authors. This ignited a desire within me to gather and compile information on plants that our ancestors used in Noongar country. My desire was to publish a document using information gathered from published records and from my own empirical knowledge, which can be used as a reference and, even more importantly, a historical record for all our Noongar people.

With the assistance of John, I believe that our first book is a unique body of work. We have only covered the bare minimum of plants in Noongar country but we both would love to see this work encourage other Noongar people to do the same and in so doing broaden the knowledge about our beautiful culture and country so that it won't be lost.

Sharing cultural knowledge is an important aspect of my life and I really enjoy having the opportunities to pass the knowledge on to my family and the wider community. I also draw a great deal of pleasure from seeing how my work benefits others especially in improving their health and well-being.

Nowadays I am often accompanied by family members, especially my young grandchildren and great grandchildren, when we return to the places where I grew up. I share my stories with them, thereby ensuring that my knowledge is passed down to the next generation.

I attribute my passion and knowledge of bush tucker and bush medicine to my grandparents and family elders in the early stages of my life and the ongoing support of my husband Morton and family. All of my knowledge is based on my interpretation of Noongar practices handed down to me by my ancestors.

John's Story

My first contact with an Australian Indigenous community was in 1963 when I spent two years with the Warnindilyakwa people, who speak the Anindilyakwa language, on Groote Eylandt in the Northern Territory, Australia. I was employed by BHP and later Groote Eylandt Mining Company but spent many hours on my days off hunting and fishing with the men of the island and learning how to prepare and cook the bush tucker. While on the island I couldn't help noticing how fit and healthy the Warnindilyakwa people were. Although the people lived at the Anglican missions at Angurugu and Umbakumba, they often spent long periods away from the missions hunting, fishing, crabbing, gathering bush tucker

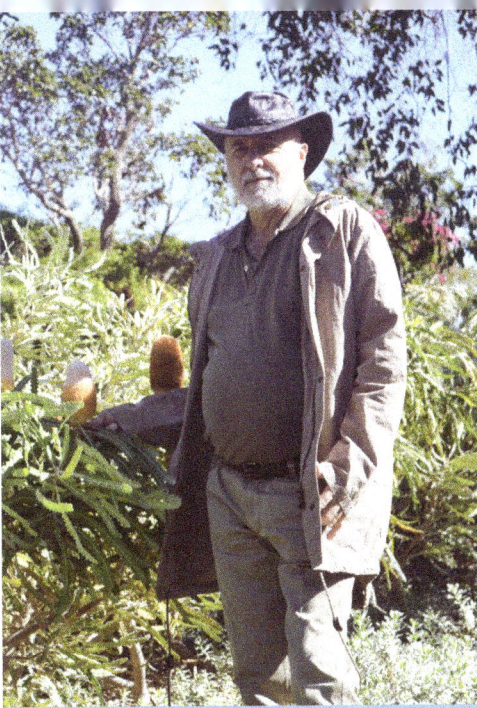

John Horsfall

and medicinal plants and getting plenty of exercise doing so. One of the last jobs of my long career in nursing and teaching was working at Curtin University's Centre for Aboriginal Studies in the Indigenous Community Health Program. The aim of the program was to teach Aboriginal students how to plan, develop, manage and evaluate community primary health care programs that promoted a healthier lifestyle for Aboriginal communities. This of course included promoting a healthier diet and getting people away from fast foods, processed foods and drink with lots of sugar, and getting them back to a more traditional, precolonisation diet of lean meat, seafood, grains, root and green vegetables and fruit.

Trees, Shrubs, Bushes and Other Plants

All trees, shrubs, bushes and other plants listed in this section are native to the south-west of Western Australia. There are other plants with edible parts in the south-west of Western Australia, but they have been introduced since colonisation and are not native to this area, so will not be discussed in this book.

Caution

All native plants are protected in Western Australia by law. You need a licence to take part or all of any native plant in the wild on Crown land. If you wish to grow any Western Australian native plants at home, there are wildflower nurseries that cater to this need. Please do not pick any wildflowers or dig up any plants without a licence.

Catspaw (*Anigozanthos humilis*)

Acacias
(Wuanga, Mindaleny and Mindalong)

There are 1,380 species of Acacia in the world and Australia has about 985 of them. Their habitats range fron rainforest areas to the more arid inland areas. The largest numbers of Acacias are found in the coastal, near coastal and the semi-arid wheatbelt regions of Western Australia. Acacias range in size from mat-like creepers to tall trees, but most are shrubs or small trees between 1 to 5 metres high (World Wide Wattle, 2016). Their bright yellow flowers are either globe shaped or cylindrical. Some Acacias flower throughout the year although the bulk of them flower during spring and summer (Djilba to Birak) and a few flower during autumn and winter (Late Buburu to Djeran) (Australian National Botanic Gardens, 2018).

The more useful species of Acacias are listed in the following table.

Family Fabaceae Lindl.

Common Names	Botanical Name	Noongar Names	Distribution
Desert Carpet	*Acacia redolens* Maslin.	Berrung (a generic Noongar name for a low, flowering shrub) (City of Joondalup, 2011)	Avon Wheatbelt to Esperance
Jam Wattle, Raspberry Jam Tree, Fine Leaf Jam, Raspberry Jam and Jam Tree	*Acacia acuminata* Benth.	Mungart, Mangart, Manjart, Munert, Munertor, Mungaitch, Mungat and Mungut (Abbott, 1983)	Geraldton to Esperance and east to Kalgoorlie
Manna Wattle	*Acacia microbotrya* Benth.	Paadyang, Mindalong (Wheatbelt NRM, 2009), Badjong, Galyang, Koonert, Kunart, Kwonnat, Men and Menna (Abbott, 1983)	Avon Wheatbelt to Albany
Orange Wattle, Blue-leafed Wattle, Golden Wreath Wattle, Kudjong and Western Australian Golden Wattle	*Acacia saligna* (Labill.) H.L.Wendl	Coojong, Cujong, Kalyung, Kileyung, Kudjong (City of Joondalup, 2011) and Biytch (Moore, 1884b)	Geraldton to Esperance
Panjang	*Acacia lasiocarpa* Benth.	Panjang	Geraldton to Esperance
Prickly Moses	*Acacia pulchella* R.Br	Mindaleny (Perth Region NRM, 2015)	Geraldton to Esperance
Red-eyed Wattle, Cyclops Wattle, One-eyed Wattle, Red-eye, Red Wreath Acacia and Western Coastal Wattle	*Acacia cyclops* G.Don	Munyuret, Woolya Wah, Wilyawa (City of Joondalup, n.d.) and Bulyee (Explore Melville, 2012)	Around the coast from Geraldton to western Victoria

Common Names	Botanical Name	Noongar Names	Distribution
Rigid Wattle	*Acacia cochlearis* (Labill.) H.L.Wendl	Galyang (Moore, 1884b)	Lancelin to Esperance
Umbrella Bush, Small Cooba, Sandhill Wattle, Marpoo, Dune Wattle, Small Coobah and Wirra	*Acacia ligulata* Benth. (also known as *Acacia bivenosa subsp. wayi* and *Acacia salicina var. wayi*)	Not known	Occurs in all states and territories except Tasmania
White-stemmed Wattle	*Acacia xanthina* Benth.	Not known	Along the coast from Shark Bay to Perth
Wiry Wattle	*Acacia extensa* Lindl	Not known	Perth to Albany

Culinary Uses Noongars mixed the gum (kalyang) of the Jam Wattle with water to make a drink called Djilyan. The gum oozing from wounds in the trunks of the Orange Wattle, Jam Wattle, Manna Wattle and Ridgid Wattle can be eaten. The pale gum is the best as the darker gum is reported to be too astringent (Low, 1991; Moore, 1884b). The seeds of the Desert Carpet, Manna Wattle, Orange Wattle, Panjang, Prickly Moses, Red-eyed Wattle, Rigid Wattle, Umbrella Bush, White-stemmed Wattle and Wiry Wattle were pounded to make flour, which was then used to make damper, a bread that Noongars call mereny (City of Joondalup, 2011; Daw et al, 2011; Meagher, 1974; SERCUL, 2014). The gum oozing from wounds of Red-eyed Wattle also made good chewing gum (City of Joondalup, 2011; Daw et al, 2011; SERCUL, 2014). Grubs (bardi) that inhabit the root system of some Acacias (e.g. Red-eyed Wattle and Umbrella Bush) can be eaten raw or roasted (SERCUL, 2014).

Other Uses The gum of the Jam Wattle (menna) was eaten to treat diarrhoea and to aid digestion. The flowers were crushed, and the vapours inhaled to relax the mind for a good night's sleep. Weak infusions of the flowers of Jam Wattle were used as a wash for blisters and burns to aid healing. An infusion or decoction (tea) of the bark (boort) of the Umbrella Bush was used as a cough medicine and as a wash for burns. The ash of this shrub was mixed with the native tobacco Pituri (*Duboisia hopwoodii*) for chewing (Lassak & McCarthy, 2008). Bindon (1996) relates that a decoction of the bark of the Umbrella Bush was also used as a general treatment for 'dizziness, nerves and fits' and that the branches were used to 'smoke people for general sickness and women following childbirth'. The juice of the leaves of Red-eyed Wattle extracted by crushing them was used as an insect repellent, sunscreen and for relieving eczema (City of Joondalup, 2011; Yelakitj Moort Noongar Association Inc., 2008).

Jam Wattle (*Acacia acuminata*)

Orange Wattle (*Acacia saligna*)

Red-eyed Wattle (*Acacia cyclops*)

Umbrella Bush (*Acacia ligulata*)

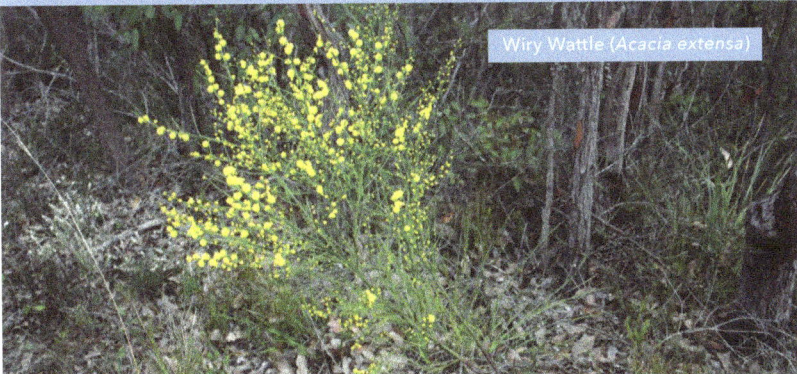

Wiry Wattle (*Acacia extensa*)

Annual Bluebell

Botanical Name *Wahlenbergia gracilenta* Lothian.

Other Common Name Hairy Annual Bluebell.

Noongar Name Not known.

Field Notes Annual Bluebell is an erect, hairy, annual herb that grows to 40 cm in height. It has ovate leaves to 40 mm long that become sparser, narrower and lanceolate towards the top of the stems. Its blue, bell-shaped flowers with five petals appear from May to December (Djeran to Djilba). Annual Bluebells grow in a variety of soils on granite outcrops, winter-wet depressions and hillsides. They are a native of Western Australia and grow all over the south-west from Shark Bay to Israelite Bay (FloraBase, 2018). They are also found in South Australia, New South Wales, Victoria and Tasmania (Atlas of Living Australia, 2018).

Culinary Uses The flowers are edible and were probably eaten by Aboriginal groups across the southern half of Australia (Yarra Ranges, 2010a).

Family Campanulaceae Juss.

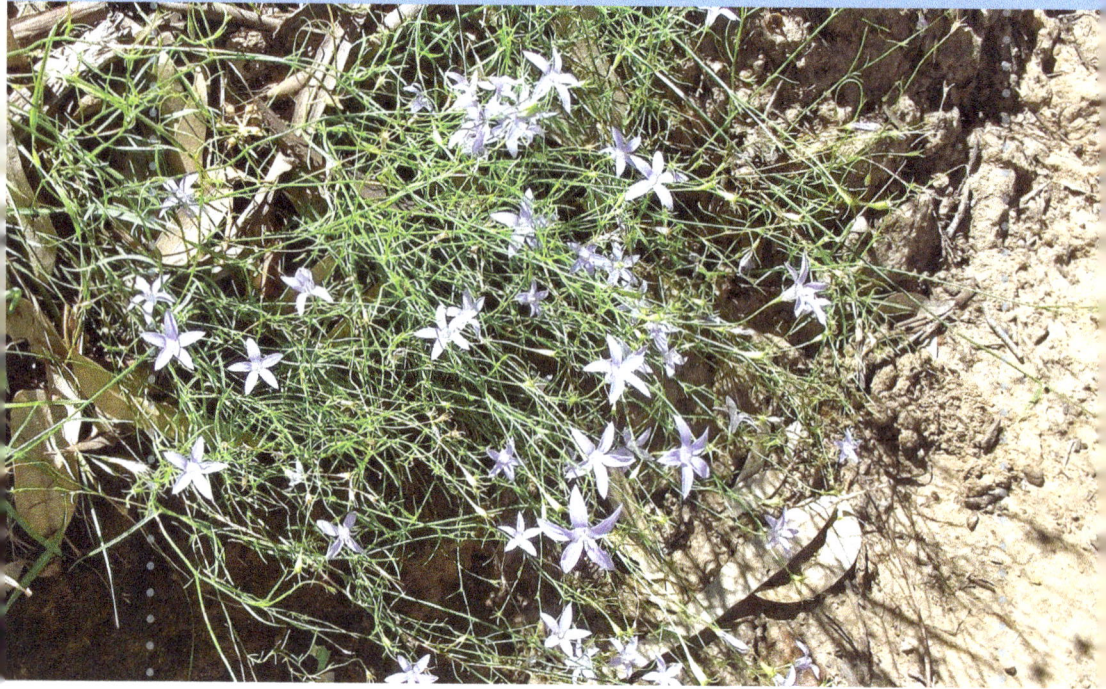

Botanical Name *Wahlenbergia stricta* (R.Br.) Sweet.

Other Common Names Australian Bluebell and Tall Bluebell.

Noongar Name Not known.

Field Notes Austral Bluebell is a clumping, much branched, perennial herb that grows to around 50 cm in height. Its leaves are linear, hairy and ovate with wavy edges and are up to 70 mm long. Its flowers are blue open bells that are present in spring and summer (late Djilba to Birak). Austral Bluebell is found in various habitats in all states of Australia except the Northern Territory (Herman, 2001). It is native to the south-west of Western Australia where it grows from Perth to Albany (FloraBase, 2018).

Culinary Uses The flowers are edible and were probably eaten by Aboriginal groups across the southern half of Australia (Herman, 2001).

Family Campanulaceae Juss.

Family Convolvulaceae Juss.

Botanical Name *Convolvulus angustissimus* R.Br.

Noongar Name Not known.

Field Notes Australian Bindweed is a perennial plant, with a trailing or twining nature, that grows to around 0.6 m high. In Western Australia, its pink or white trumpet-shaped flowers can be seen all year round. This plant grows in a variety of soils including sandy loams, red sands, clay and limestone, in damp areas and on slopes (FloraBase, 2018). In Western Australia it grows in coastal and near-coastal areas between Geraldton and the South Australian border. It also grows in all other Australian states except the Northern Territory (Australian Native Plants Society (Australia), 2018).

Culinary Uses The roots (bwoor) of this plant can be eaten. Because the root is tough and starchy Aboriginal people

usually cooked and kneaded the root pulp into dough before eating it (De Angeles, 2005; Gott, 2010).

Family Pittosporaceae R.Br.

Botanical Name *Billardiera heterophylla* (Lindl.) L.Cayzer and Crisp.

Other Common Name Bluebell Creeper.

Noongar Name Gumug, Kuruba and Namman (Meagher, 1975).

Field Notes The Australian Bluebell is a climbing plant that likes to twist around the stems of a host plant for support. Its bright green, lanceolate leaves are about 5 cm long. The blue, white or pink bell-shaped flowers, from where it gets its name, have five petals. They appear from December to February (Birak to Bunuru). The Australian Bluebell prefers sandy soils and tolerates soils with high salinity. It is found in coastal areas and around inland salt lakes from Cervantes to Esperance (FloraBase, 2018). Its edible fruits are cylindrical, around 20 mm long and are a greenish-blue to dark-blue in

colour when ripe (Australian Native Plants Society (Australia), 2018; Daw et al, 2011).

Culinary Uses Noongars ate the ripe, fleshy fruits, which are reportedly quite sweet with a soft texture (Daw et al, 2011; Gott, 2015).

Botanical Name *Billardiera fusiformis* Labill.

Other Common Names Australian Blue-bell, Bluebell Creeper, Native Bluebell, Purple Appleberry, Sollya, Western Australian Bluebell, West Australian Bluebell Creeper and Western Australian Bluebell Creeper (Weeds of Australia, 2011).

Noongar Names Cummock and Kummuck, (Greenskills, n.d.) and Gumug (SERCUL, 2014).

Field Notes The Australian Bluebell Creeper is a climbing plant or creeper. It has bright green, leathery, ovate leaves and blue, white or pink bell-shaped flowers that appear from November to February (Kambarang to Bunuru). Its cylindrical fruits are dark green to purplish in colour and are up to 20 mm long. This climber prefers coastal and near coastal

forests and is indigenous to the south-west of Western Australia from Cervantes to Israelite Bay (FloraBase, 2018).

Culinary Uses The plant's blue berries (karlburi) are quite fleshy and are a rich source of Vitamin C. The fruit can be eaten when they turn a pink, transparent colour (Greenskills, n.d.; SERCUL, 2014).

Family Solanaceae Juss.

Botanical Name *Lycium australe* F.Muell.

Noongar Name Not known.

Field Notes Australian Boxthorn is a spiny shrub that grows to 2.5 m in height. Its greyish-green, thick and fleshy leaves are narrowly obovoid to ellipsoid and are up to 25 mm in length. Its white-cream or blue-purple flowers have four petals. They appear from February to October (Bunuru to early Kambarang). Its dull orange-red berries are ovoid to ellipsoid and are from 2–5 mm in diameter.

Australian Boxthorn is usually found in sandy and clayey soils on the edges of salt lakes and claypans (FloraBase, 2018) right across the southern half of Australia (Atlas of Living Australia, 2018).

Culinary Uses The berries of the Australian Boxthorn are edible when ripe (Clarke, 1985).

Botanical Name *Daucus glochidiatus* (Labill.) Fisch., C.A.Mey. and Ave-Lall.

Other Common Names Austral Carrot and Native Carrot.

Noongar Names Kwordiny (Wheatbelt NRM, n.d.) and Mongming (Goode et al, 2010).

Field Notes The Australian Carrot is a slender annual plant that grows to around 0.6 m high. Its pinnate leaves have ovate segments and are approximately 5 cm long. Its flowers can be pink, purplish, white or a yellow-green colour. They appear from August to January (Djilba to late Birak). In Western Australia, this plant is found in a variety of soils around the coast and inland from Karratha all over the south-west around to the South Australian border. (FloraBase, 2018). It is also found in all other Australian states. (Atlas of Living Australia, 2018)

Family Apiaceae Lindl.

Culinary Uses The slender carrot-like root (bwoor) of the Australian Carrot is edible (Wheatbelt NRM, n.d.).

Family Malvaceae Juss.

Botanical Name *Malva preissiana* Miq., formerly *Lavatera plebeia*.

Other Common Name Native Marshmallow.

Noongar Name Not known.

Field Notes The Australian Hollyhock is an annual or biennial, sturdy, erect shrub that grows to around 2 m high. The ovate or kidney-shaped leaves are approximately 60 mm long. Its flowers are approximately 50 mm across and white in the Perth region, but inland they may be mauve (Rippey and Rowland, 1995). Australian Hollyhock grows in a variety of soils and habitats on 'rocky islands, stony plains, flat valley floors and road verges' (FloraBase, 2018). The Australian Hollyhock is found on the south-west coastal strip and on islands, from Dirk Hartog Island to Busselton. An inland variant can be found from Coolgardie through

South Australia, Victoria, New South Wales and southern Queensland (Rippey and Rowland, 1995).

Culinary Uses The roots (bwoor) are edible and are reported to have a parsnip-like consistency (Cribb and Cribb, 1987; Maiden, 1889; Rippey and Rowland, 2004). The fresh flowers are also edible (Lassak and McCarthy, 2008).

Other Uses Infusions (teas) of the fresh flowers were taken internally for digestive tract, respiratory and urinary tract inflammation (Rippey and Rowland, 1995). Poultices of the boiled leaves were used to treat sores and boils (Lassak and McCarthy, 2008).

Botanical Name *Pterostylis vittata* Lindl.

Other Common Name Green-banded Greenhood Orchid.

Noongar Name Kararr (City of Joondalup, 2011).

Field Notes The Banded Greenhood Orchid is a tuberous, perennial orchid that only grows to around 0.45 m high. Nonflowering plants have a basal rosette of leaves, but flowering plants do not produce them. Its flowers are an unusual green with white stripes. They appear from May to September (late Djeran to Djilba). It grows in a variety of soils in coastal and near-coastal situations from Geraldton to Israelite Bay (FloraBase, 2018).

Family Orchidaceae Juss.

Culinary Uses Noongars either roasted or baked the tuberous roots (bwoor) of the Banded Greenhood in hot ashes or pounded the flesh of the root into a paste and made cakes that they baked in hot ashes (City of Joondalup, 2011).

Banksias (Bwongka)

The Banksias were named after Sir Joseph Banks (1743–1820), a prominent naturalist and botanist who was on the *Endeavour* with Captain James Cook on his voyage to the east coast of Australia in 1770.

Some plants in the Banksia genus were originally listed under the Dryandra genus. The Western Australian Herbarium state on their FloraBank website: 'The Western Australian Herbarium has recently changed the names of all species of Dryandra to an equivalent name in Banksia, to reflect a taxonomic change in which the two genera have been merged into one.' They go on to say that, 'Two botanists, Kevin Thiele from the Western Australian Herbarium and Austin Mast from the University of Florida, recently published a paper with strong evidence that Dryandras are actually a subgroup of Banksia rather than a genus in their own right.'

Banksias, with one exception, are only found in Australia. Sixty of the Australian Banksias are endemic to the south-west of Western Australia. The eastern and western Banksias are quite separate species (Australian National Botanic Gardens, 2018). Most Banksias in Western Australia flower in the spring and early summer (Djilba to Birak). The table lists the more prominent Banksias that are endemic to the south-west of Western Australia.

Common Name	Botanical Name	Noongar Name	Distribution
Acorn Banksia	*Banksia prionotes* Lindl.	Manyret	Kalbarri to Katanning
Banksia fraseri (no generally accepted common name)	*Banksia fraseri* (R.Br.) A.R.Mast and K.R.Thiele	Budjan and Butyak (Moore, 1884a)	Kalbarri to Katanning
Bird's Nest Banksia	*Banksia baxteri* R.Br.	Not known	Albany to Esperance
Bull Banksia	*Banksia grandis* Willd.	Mungite, Poolgarla (City of Joondalup, 2011), Mangij, Mungytch (Pibulmun for the flower) (Greenskills, n.d.) and Beera	Perth to Albany
Couch Honeypot	*Banksia dallanneyi* A.R.Mast and K.R.Thiele	Bulgalla (Abbott, 1983) and Yonga Kwan	Kalbarri to Albany
Dryandra-leaved Banksia	*Banksia dryandroides* Sweet	Manyat (Abbott, 1983)	Albany to Bremer Bay
Firewood Banksia	*Banksia menziesii* R.Br.	Mungyte and Mungite (City of Joondalup, 2011)	Kalbarri to Bunbury
Quairading Banksia	*Banksia cuneata* A.S.George	Not known	Around Quairading

Common Name	Botanical Name	Noongar Name	Distribution
Parrot Bush	*Banksia sessilis* (Knight) A.R.Mast and K.R.Thiele (formerly *Dryandra sessilis*)	Pulgart (City of Joondalup, 2011), Budjan (Abbott, 1983) and Pudjak	Kalbarri to Bremer Bay
Red Swamp Banksia	*Banksia occidentalis* R.Br.	Mo, Yundill (Abbott, 1983), Mangatj and Pia	Cape Naturaliste to Israelite Bay
Round-fruit Banksia	*Banksia sphaerocarpa* R.Br.	Nugoo (Meagher, 1975)	Geraldton to Albany and inland to Southern Cross
Scarlet Banksia	*Banksia coccinea* R.Br.	Waddib (Abbott, 1983)	Albany to Esperance
Slender Banksia	*Banksia attenuata* R.Br	Piara, Biara, Bealwra, Peera, Piras (City of Joondalup, 2011) and Binda (Abbott, 1983)	Kalbarri to Hopetoun
Southern Plains Banksia	*Banksia media* R.Br.	Not known	Albany to Cape Arid
Swamp Banksia	*Banksia littoralis* R.Br.	Pungura (Bennett, 1991), Boongura (Abbott, 1983), Boora, Boorarup and Mimidi	Cervantes to Bremer Bay
Urchin Dryandra	*Banksia undata* A.R.Mast and K.R.Thiele	Bwongka (Birdlife Australia, n.d.)	Swan Coastal Plain and hills area
Woolly Banksia	*Banksia baueri* R.Br.	Mangatj (Wheat-belt NRM, 2009)	Avon Wheatbelt, Western Mallee and Esperance

Parrot Bush (*Banksia sessilis*)

Culinary Uses The Banksias were a great source of nectar (djidja or ngonyang) for Noongars, who either sucked the nectar directly from the flowers or made a sweet, refreshing drink (mangite or mungitch) by soaking the flower spikes of Banksias in water (Maiden, 1889). The Noongar verb to steep in water is Nyogulang (Moore, 1884b). Sometimes the resulting liquid was left to ferment into an intoxicating drink called gep (City of Joondalup, 2011). The sweet liquid was also used medicinally as a cough mixture and to sooth a sore throat (Hansen and Horsfall, 2016).

Other Uses The cones (metjokoondail) of some Banksias, such as the Slender Banksia (Piara) and the Firewood Banksia (Mungyte), were used by Noongars as torches to carry fire from one campsite to the next (City of Joondalup, 2011).

Quairading Banksia (*Banksia cuneata*)

Red Swamp Banksia (*Banksia occidentalis*)

Scarlet Banksia (*Banksia coccinea*)

Southern Plains Banksia (*Banksia media*)

Family Chenopodiaceae Vent.

Botanical Name *Enchylaena tomentosa* R.Br.

Other Common Name Ruby Saltbush.

Noongar Name Not known.

Field Notes Barrier Saltbush grows as a prostrate or erect shrub to around 0.6 m in height. Its cylindrical, semi-succulent leaves are up to 2 cm long. Both leaves and stems are covered in hairs. Its small, insignificant flowers appear from May to September (late Djeran to Djilba). It bears edible, button-like fruits that are bright red when ripe. The plant grows in a variety of soils both around the coast and inland (FloraBase, 2018). It is found in all Australian states except Tasmania, both in sub-tropical and more temperate regions. (Australian National Botanic Gardens, 2018)

Culinary Uses The succulent, button-shaped berries (karlburi) are red when ripe. They were eaten fresh as a snack food or dried and soaked in water and reconstituted later (Cribb and Cribb, 1987; De Angeles, 2005; Gott, 2010). The fruits have a black stone inside that is also edible (Australian National Botanic Gardens, 2018). The leaves can be boiled or steamed and eaten (Low, 1991).

Botanical Name *Salicornia quinqueflora* Ung.-Sternb.

Noongar Name Milyu is the generic Noongar name for Samphire (Moore, 1884a; Parks and Wildlife Service, 2018).

Field Notes Beaded Samphire is a perennial plant or shrub that starts off prostrate but becomes upright, later growing to around 0.5 m high. It flowers in February (early Bunuru). It prefers sandy soils or clay but tolerates moderately saline soils. It is found near swamps, estuaries and salt lakes in coastal and near-coastal situations from Shark Bay to Israelite Bay on the south coast (FloraBase, 2018).

Culinary Uses The leaves and young shoots of Beaded Samphire can be eaten raw, boiled or steamed, but can be a bit salty. It is suggested that the boiled leaves might be more palatable if water is changed at least once (Cribb and Cribb, 1987; Kapitany, 2015).

Berry Saltbush

Botanical Name *Atriplex semibaccata* R.Br.

Other Common Names Australian Saltbush and Creeping Saltbush.

Noongar Name Not known.

Field Notes Berry Saltbush grows as a low groundcover to 15 cm in height and 3 m in diameter. Its grey leaves are approximately 1.5 cm long and they have wavy edges. Its small, greenish flowers occur in mid summer (Birak). After flowering red berries appear (Indigenous Flora and Fauna Association, n.d.). Berry Saltbush prefers saline flats and lakes. It is native in parts to the south-west of Western Australia and is found from Geraldton to Esperance and east as far as Kalgoorlie (FloraBase, 2018). It is also found in southern Queensland, New South Wales, Victoria, South Australia and on the east coast of Tasmania (Atlas of Living Australia, 2018).

Family Chenopodiaceae Vent.

Culinary Uses The berries of Berry Saltbush when ripe are red and juicy and are edible but slightly salty (Williams and Sides, 2008).

Botanical Name *Santalum murrayanum* (T.Mitch.) C.A.Gardner

Noongar Name Kulya, Tjak (Wheatbelt NRM, 2015) and Coolyar (Abbott, 1989).

Field Notes Bitter Quandong is a weeping tree that grows to around 5 m in height. The lanceolate leaves have a hooked tip and are pale, yellowish green in colour and around 3.5 cm long. The fruits are about 2 cm in diameter and mature to a green-yellow or pale orange colour. The fruit contains a large seed with an edible kernel. The plant grows across southern Australia. In Western Australia it grows south of a line drawn from Perth to Kalgoorlie (Archer, 2018).

Culinary Uses Noongars ate the seed kernels after roasting them. They also ate the roasted bark (boort) of the roots (bwoor) in inland areas where food was scarcer (Cribb and Cribb, 1987; Low, 1991).

Family Santalaceae R.Br.

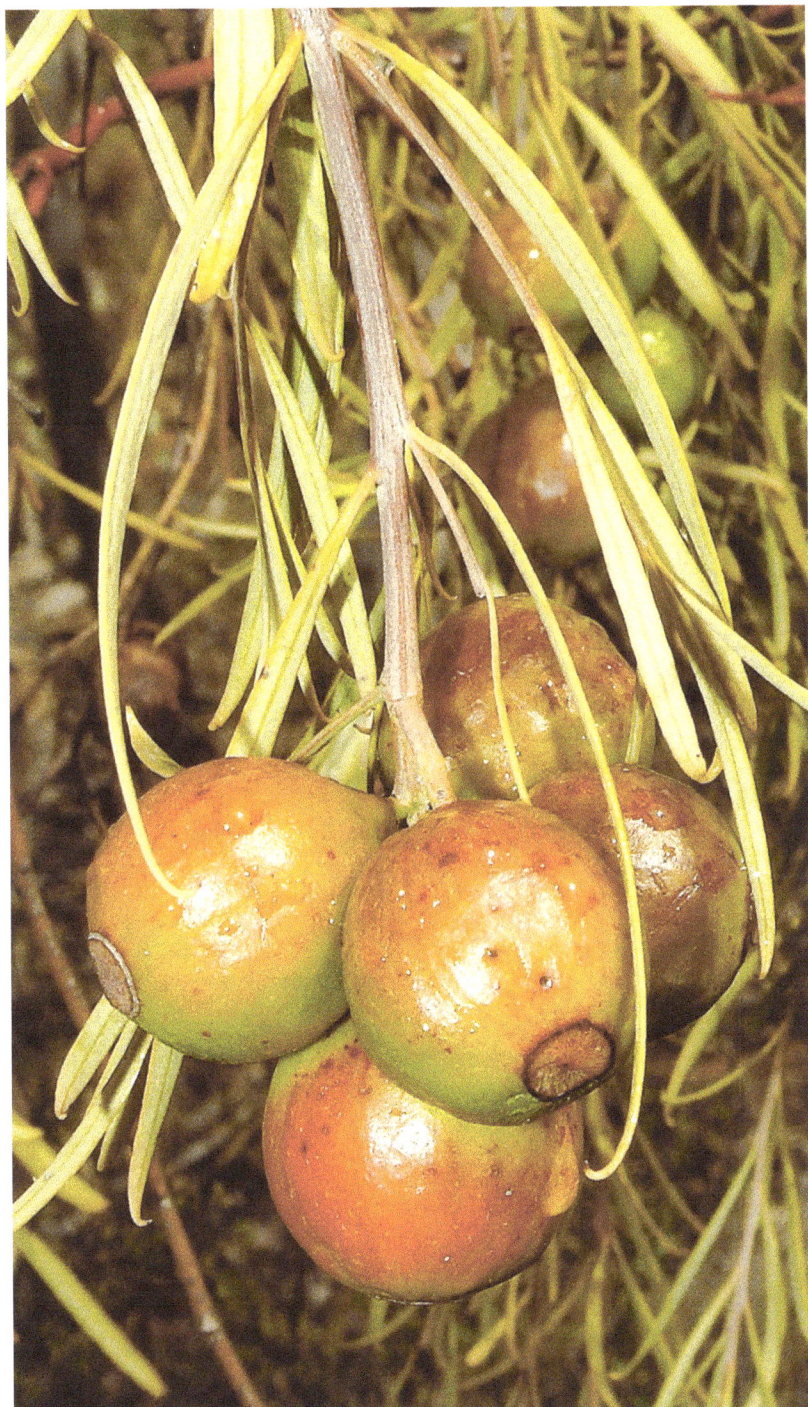

Botanical Name *Tecticornia pergranulata* (J.M.Black) K.A.Sheph. & Paul G.Wilson, formerly *Halosarcia pergranulata*.

Other Common Names Blackseed Glasswort and Beadbush.

Noongar Name Milyu is the generic Noongar name for Samphire (Moore, 1884a; Parks and Wildlife Service, 2018)

Field Notes Blackseed Samphire is a succulent shrub that grows to about 1 m in height. The stems are segmented and don't have leaves. The small branchlets that arise from the main stems are made of small bead-shaped segments about 3 mm long. The plant produces small flowers in spring and early summer (Djilba to early Birak). After flowering, fruiting spikes appear containing brown or black round seeds. The plant can tolerate soils with a high saline content (Oz Native Plants, 2018). Blackseed Samphire is found all over the south-west of Western Australia from Geraldton to Esperance and out beyond Kalgoorlie (FloraBase, 2018).

Culinary Uses The young stems of Blackseed Samphire are reported to be edible. They are said to be crisp and taste a little salty (Mary River Catchment and Coordinating Committee, 2014).

Family Chenopodiaceae Vent.

Family Haemodoraceae R.Br.

Botanical Names *Haemodorum spicatum* R.Br. *Haemodorum simulans* F.Muell. and *Haemodorum paniculatum* Lindl.

Noongar Names Mardja, Boon, Bhon (Meagher, 1975); Matje (Bennett, 1991; Abbott, 1983) Bohrn, Djanbar, (Moore, 1884b), Koolung, Quirting (Bindon and Chadwick, 1992) (*Haemodorum spicatum*), Mutta (*Haemodorum simulans*), Mardja (Meagher, 1975) and Madja (Moore, 1884b) (*Haemodorum paniculatum*).

Field Notes There are three Bloodroots that are found in the south-west of Western Australia. They are small plants that usually produce two or three 60 cm round, tough, green leaves each year, which stay alive to form a series of leaves with next year's lot. A single flower spike (rarely two) emerges each year from October to January (Kambarang to Birak).

The spikes grow to around 1 m in height. The stems and the flowers are dark brown to black in colour (Archer, 2018). Bloodroots like coastal or near-coastal situations with sandy or sandy clay soils. *Haemodorum spicatum* and *Haemodorum simulans* are prolific from Geraldton to Esperance, whereas *Haemodorum paniculatum* is only found on the Geraldton and Perth sandplains (FloraBase, 2018).

Culinary Uses The red-coloured bulbous roots (bwoor) of all three Bloodroots are edible and are said to taste a bit spicy with a mild onion flavour. The bulbs were a staple part of the Noongar diet in the south-west and were eaten raw or roasted on hot coals (Daw et al, 2011; Greenskills, n.d.; Maiden, 1889; Moore, 1884b). Sometimes the roasted roots were ground and mixed with more bland foods to make them tastier (Coppin, 2008; Explore Melville, 2012; SERCUL, 2014).

Other Uses The roots and leaf bases were roasted and pounded with clay from termite nests and then eaten to stop diarrhoea in dysentery (Lassak and McCarthy, 2001). Decoctions (teas) of the bulb (made by boiling them in water) were drunk to relieve lung congestion. The bulbs pounded into a paste were rubbed into the body for arthritis. A paste made from the bulb was used to treat toothache and mouth ulcers.

Family Hemerocallidaceae R.Br.

Botanical Name *Dianella revoluta* R.Br.

Other Common Names Blueberry Lily, Spreading Flax-lily and Black-anther Flax-lily.

Noongar Names Mangard (SERCUL, 2014) and Mangarel (Perth Region NRM, 2015).

Field Notes The Blue Flax-lily is a small, clumping, drought-resistant plant that grows to around 1 m tall and spreads to around 1.5 metres. It has long, leafy, grass-like stems that are glossy green and leathery in appearance. The plant produces small, bell-shaped, purple or blue flowers that are around 10 mm long. The flowers appear in late spring to summer (Birak to Bunuru). The fruits are globular and purple (SERCUL, 2014). The Blue Flax-lily grows in a variety of soils and situations and is indigenous to the south-west of Western Australia, as well as the southern reaches of South

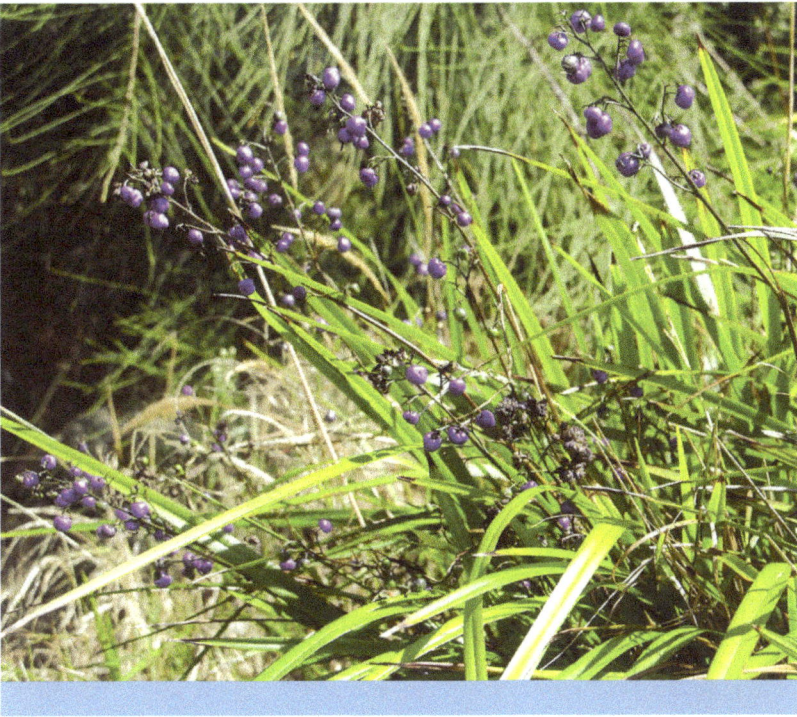

Australia, Victoria, New South Wales, Tasmania and south-east Queensland (Australian National Botanic Gardens, 2018).

Culinary Uses Both the fruit and the roots (bwoor) of this shrub are edible, although the fruits are reportedly a bit salty and slightly bitter. Noongars either ate the roots raw, roasted in hot ashes, or steamed in an earth oven (City of Joondalup, 2011; Perth Region NRM, n.d.b; SERCUL, 2014; Wildflower Society of WA, n.d.).

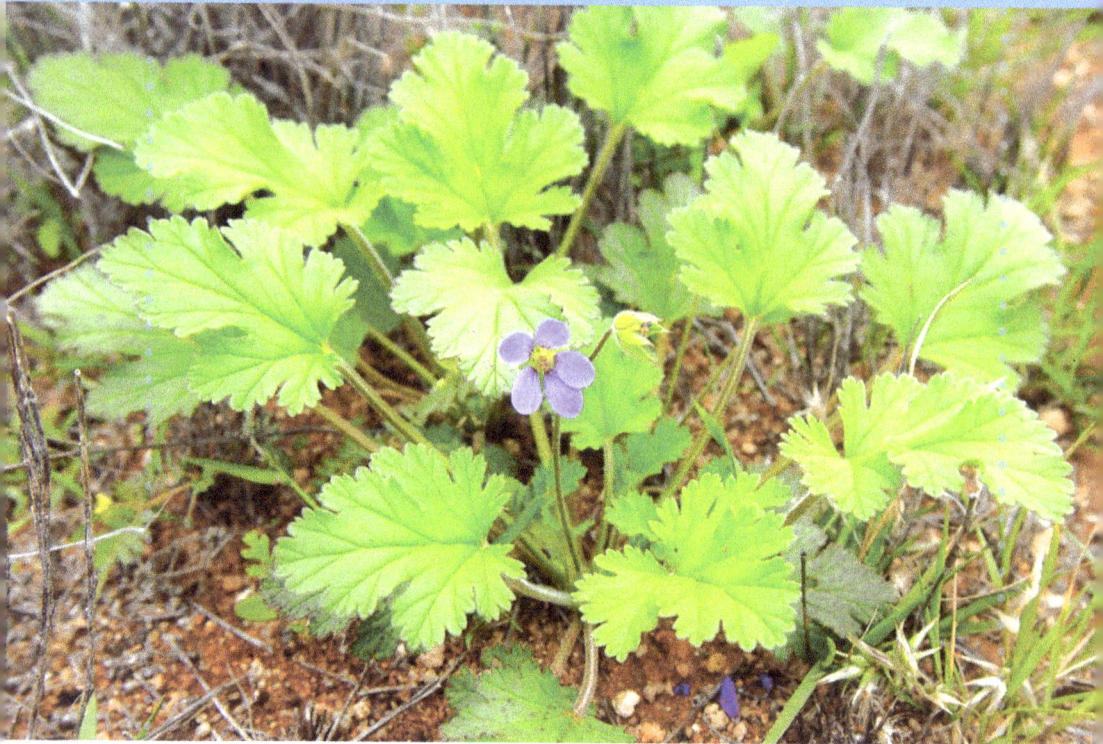

Botanical Name *Erodium cygnorum* Nees.

Other Common Names Blue Storksbill and Pinweed.

Noongar Name Not known.

Field Notes Blue Heronsbill is a small annual or perennial plant that grows to around 0.6 m high. It has green leaves with three lobes and bright blue or pink flowers with five petals that appear from July to October (late Makuru to early Kambarang). It thrives in sandy or clay loam in a variety of habitats all over the southern portion of Western Australia south of Karratha (FloraBase, 2018). It is also found in the southern parts of the Northern Territory and Queensland and all over South Australia, Victoria and New South Wales (Atlas of Living Australia, 2018).

Family Geraniaceae Juss.

Culinary Uses The entire plant is edible and is reported to taste like parsley if picked young (Terra Perma Design, 2013).

Blue Squill

Family Xanthorrhoeaceae Dumort

Botanical Name *Chamaescilla corymbosa* (R.Br.) Benth.

Other Common Name Blue Stars.

Noongar Name Not known.

Field Notes Blue Squill is a small plant that grows to around 15 cm in height. It has tuberous roots (bwoor) and long sword-like leaves. Its bright blue, star-shaped flowers have six petals. They appear from July to December (late Makuru to early Birak). The flowers reportedly only last a day. The plant is found in a variety of habitats all over the south-west corner of Western Australia. It is also found in New South Wales, Victoria and Tasmania (FloraBase, 2018; Pacific Bulb Society, 2012).

Culinary Uses This plant has several small, edible tubers (De Angeles, 2005; Gott, 2010). Archer (2018) relates that,

'Aborigines would eat the tubers (about the size of a child's little finger) that are easily gathered with a digging stick as they are often numerous and near the surface'. He goes on to say, 'The ones I have sampled (after the plant has died back to the tuber) had a starchy flavour a little like a potato and are pleasantly crunchy'.

Botanical Name *Myoporum insulare* R.Br.

Other Common Name Southern Boobialla.

Noongar Name Not known.

Field Notes The Blueberry Tree grows as a prostrate or erect shrub or tree up to 5 m high. Its white flowers have five petals and grow in clusters of up to eight flowers. Its leaves are long and lanceolate. Its flowers appear from July to February (late Makuru to early Bunuru). Its fruits are purple when ripe and globular in shape. This shrub or tree prefers coastal sandplains and is found from Shark Bay in Western Australia all around the southern coast to northern New South Wales (Australian National Botanic Gardens, 2018; FloraBase, 2018).

Family Scrophulariaceae Juss.

Culinary Uses The fruits of the Blueberry Tree are edible when ripe and are reported to taste a little bit bitter and salty (Low, 1991; Maiden, 1889).

Bower Spinach

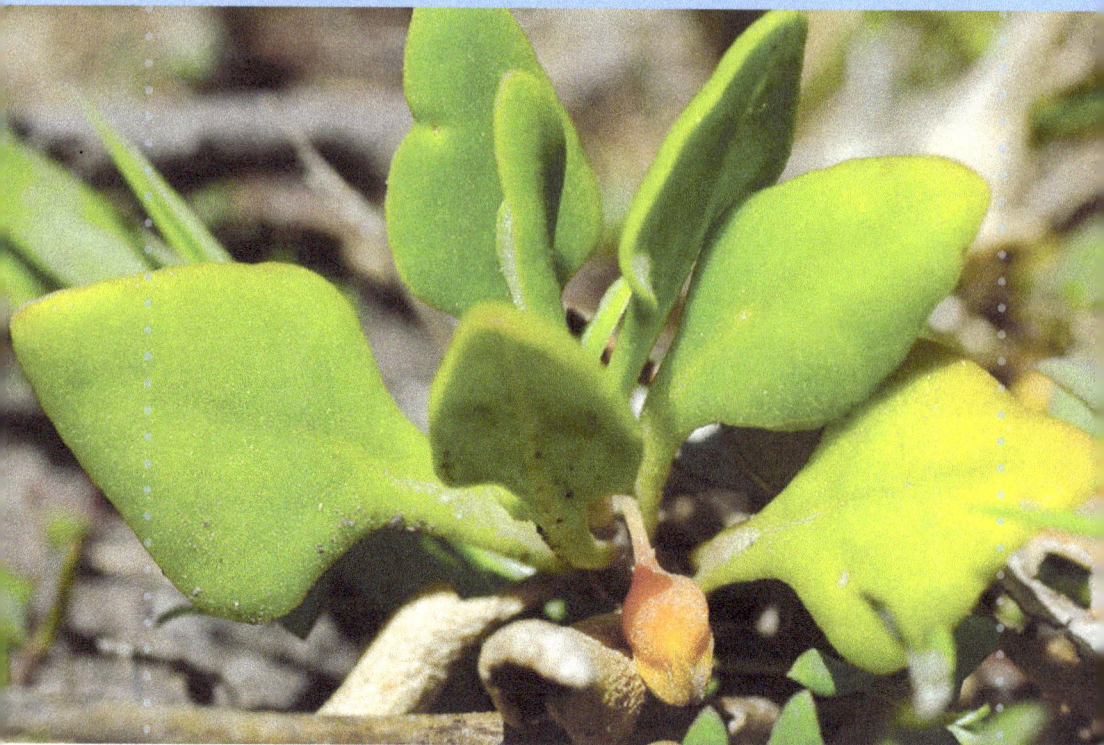

Botanical Name *Tetragonia implexicoma* (Miq.) Hook.f.

Noongar Name Not known.

Field Notes Bower Spinach is a climbing, perennial, succulent plant that climbs to approximately 0.5 m high with a 2 m spread. It has thick, succulent, ovate leaves and small, yellow, star shaped flowers with five petals. The flowers appear from February to March (Bunuru) or from May to December (late Djeran to early Birak). The small, red, spherical fruits are quite juicy. It is a very coastal plant and thrives in sandy soils (FloraBase, 2018). Bower Spinach is found right around the southern coast of Australia from Shark Bay to the Victorian Border with New South Wales (Atlas of Living Australia, 2018).

Culinary Uses Both the leaves and the fruit of Bower Spinach are edible. The fruits reportedly have a sweet, slightly

Family Aizoaceae Martinov.

salty taste. The leaves can be boiled or steamed like spinach (Coppin, 2008; Cribb and Cribb, 1987; Low, 1991).

Bracken Fern

Family Dennstaedtiaceae Lotsy

Botanical Name *Pteridium esculentum* (G.Forst.) Cockayne.

Other Common Names Bracken, Common Bracken (Bennett, 1991), Austral Fern and Austral Bracken.

Noongar Names Manya (Denmark area), Munda (Perth area), Moondan-gurnang (Abbott, 1983), Karbara and Moondark (Bindon and Chadwick, 1992).

Field Notes Bracken Fern is a perennial (everlasting) that has an extensive, creeping, hairy rhizome-type root system that allows it to spread. Its stems are up to 2.5 m long, brown and stiff, bearing large, deeply divided light green fronds that go brown as they age (HerbiGuide, 2014). Bracken Fern grows in a variety of moist soils. It is prominent in Eucalypt forests and in coastal and near coastal situations in all Australian states except the Northern Territory. In Western

Australia, it is found mostly in coastal areas from Geraldton to the South Australian border (FloraBase, 2018; Royal Botanic Gardens and Domain Trust, n.d.).

Culinary Uses The rhizomes of Bracken Fern can be eaten after they are roasted and the starchy pulp is separated from the tough inedible fibres. The fresh unfolding tips can be eaten after they are soaked in water and then dried for a few days. The hairs on the tips need to be pulled off as they can irritate the palate (Greenskills, n.d.). The young shoots emerging from the ground are also edible (Low, 1991; Maiden, 1889). There is some talk that the new green shoots contain a carcinogen that has been linked to stomach cancer so should not be consumed in big quantities if at all (Gott, 2010; Daw et al, 2011).

Other Uses Bracken Fern was used by Noongars for its medicinal properties as well as for food. Infusions (teas) of the leaves, made by steeping the crushed leaves in water, were used externally as a wash for sores and rheumatic pain. They were also taken internally for intestinal worms, including tapeworm. The juice of the young stems and crushed leaves was rubbed into the skin for insect and ant bites (Lassak and McCarthy, 2008). Infusions of the leaves and stems were applied externally as a liniment for arthritic pain (Hansen and Horsfall, 2016).

Botanical Name *Drosera macrantha* Endl.

Other Common Name Climbing Sundew.

Noongar Name: Boon (Meagher, 1975).

Field Notes Bridal Rainbow is a tuberous, perennial, climbing plant that grows to around 1.5 m in height. It has small, cup-shaped carnivorous leaves with sticky prongs and white or pink flowers with five petals that appear from June to November (Makuru to late Kambarang). Bridal Rainbow is endemic to the south-west of Western Australia and is found from Geraldton to Esperance and out as far as Wiluna (FloraBase, 2018).

Culinary Uses The small, red root (bwoor) of Bridal Rainbow was eaten raw or roasted in hot ashes. It is reported to be extremely hot and pungent and 'particularly expedient for overcoming lassitude' (Meagher, 1975).

Family Droseraceae Salisb.

Family Santalaceae R.Br.

Botanical Name *Exocarpos sparteus* R.Br.

Other Common Name Native Cherry.

Noongar Names Djuk, Chuck (Abbott, 1983; Hassell, 1975), Djiyag, Dtulya (Meagher, 1975) Weelarra and Waang (Nyungar Wardan Katitjin Bidi – Derbal Nara. n.d.).

Field Notes Broom Ballart grows as a shrub or small tree to 4 m high. Its leaves are small and fall early. The flowers are tiny and develop into edible fruits with the seed forming at the extreme end. The flower stalk is initially green turning to scarlet later (Archer, 2011). Broom Ballart is particularly widespread in Australia, occurring in all mainland states including the Northern Territory (New South Wales Flora Online, 2017). In Western Australia, it is widespread around the coastline in sandy soils but is more sporadic inland. It is

very prolific all over the south-west from Shark Bay to Israelite Bay (Archer, 2018; FloraBase, 2018).

Culinary Uses The small fruits are quite sweet when they become red and ripe (Coppin, 2008). Daw et al (2011) relate that: 'In semi-arid areas mistletoes, themselves bearing succulent orange-red fruits up to seven mm in diameter, may grow on Djuk. These taste better and give a high return of food for effort.'

Hassell (1975) observed women collecting Chuck and wrote:

> The women collected lots of this fruit for the trees bear very freely. The women's collection method was to spread their cloaks (boorks) under the tree and shake the tree well. They gathered around, ate what they wanted and took the rest back to camp.

Other Uses The leaves and twigs were burned to make smoke to repel insects. The leaves were crushed and the resulting paste was rubbed on the head to alleviate headaches.

Botanical Name *Tecticornia indica* (Willd.) K.A.Sheph. and Paul G.Wilson, formerly *Halosarcia indica*.

Noongar Name Milyu is the generic Noongar name for Samphire (Moore, 1884a; Parks and Wildlife Service, 2018).

Field Notes Brown-headed Samphire is a perennial plant with a sprawling nature that grows to around 1 m in height. Its succulent stems are leafless. Its small flowers grow to 40 mm long and form in spikes at the tops of the stems. Brown-headed Samphire is found in all Australian states except Tasmania but tends to be more prolific in moister areas around the coast and in the south-west of Western Australia (New South Wales Flora Online, 2018).

Culinary Uses The crisp, young stems of Brown-headed Samphire can be eaten and are reported to taste slightly salty (Mary River Catchment and Coordinating Committee, 2014).

Family Chenopodiaceae Vent.

Botanical Names There are two varieties of Bulrushes that grow in the south-west of Western Australia: *Typha domingensis* Pers. and *Typha orientalis* C.Presl.

Other Common Names Reedmace, Narrow Leaf Cumbungi, Narrow-leaved Cat-tail (*Typha domingensis*) and Broad-leaved Cat-tail (*Typha orientalis*).

Noongar Names Yangeti, Yanget, Lirimbi, Yanjidi, Yunjeedie, Yunjid, Tanjil, Yandijut (Bennett, 1991; Abbott, 1983) and Jetta (Moore, 1884a).

Field Notes Bulrushes are water-loving plants that grow to 3 m in height. The rhizomatous roots grow to 20 mm in diameter. The blade-like leaves of *Typha domingensis* grow to 2 m long and are around 20 mm wide. The leaves of *Typha orientalis* are a little wider. The flowers of both sexes grow on a single plant and are usually 12 to 40 cm long (Brigs, n.d.).

Family Typhaceae Juss.

The flowers appear on long stalks and are brownish in colour. They appear from May to September (late Djeran to early Djilba). Bulrushes grow around freshwater swamps, creeks or rivers (FloraBase, 2018). They grow in all states of Australia including the Northern Territory and Tasmania (Atlas of Living Australia, 2018). They are also found in other countries.

Culinary Uses The roots (bwoor) of both Bulrushes can be eaten. Noongars pounded the roots to separate the starchy pulp from the fibrous part. The resulting pulp was shaped into cakes and baked on hot coals. The centre at the base of the stem is also edible as are the very young flower spikes. Both can be eaten raw or cooked (Cribb and Cribb, 1987; Daw et al, 2011; Explore Melville, 2012; Low, 1991; Maiden, 1889; SERCUL, n.d.).

Other Uses The fibres in the tubers are quite strong and were used to make string. The dried shredded leaves made good mats and baskets. Parts of the plant are reported to have antiseptic properties. The plant was sometimes thrown into the fire as the smoke from this plant was a good insect repellent (Survival, Tracking and Awareness, 2012).

Bush Bean

Botanical Name *Rhyncharrhena linearis* (Decne.) K.L.Wilson.

Other Common Names Purple Pentatrope, Climbing Purple-star, Mulga Bean and Cocola Bean.

Noongar Name Not known.

Field Notes Bush Bean grows as a twining shrub or climber. Its linear leaves are up to 10 mm long and 6 mm wide. Its brown-purple flowers have five petals and hang on stalks. They appear from March to October (late Bunuru to early Kambarang). The long cylindrical beans or fruit are tapered at both ends and grow to 300 mm long and 8 mm wide. In Western Australia, it grows all over an area from Newman to Perth. It is found in the drier areas of all other states except Tasmania (Atlas of Living Australia, 2017; FloraBase, 2018; Flora NT, 2018).

Culinary Uses The young beans (fruit) of the Bush Bean can be eaten whole. The seeds, when dry, can be ground to make flour for damper (Dann, 2003; Florek, 2014).

Family Apocynaceae Juss.

Candle Cranberry

Botanical Name *Astroloma ciliatum* (Lindl.) Druce.

Noongar Name Not known.

Field Notes Candle Cranberry grows as a prostrate shrub to around 0.3 m in height. It has needle-like leaves and red, tubular flowers with a black base and five small petals that appear from May to October (late Djeran to early Kambarang). Its fruit are small berries (karlburi). The Candle Cranberry is endemic to the south-west of Western Australia and is found from Cervantes to Albany (Atlas of Living Australia, 2018; FloraBase, 2018).

Culinary Uses The small berries (karlburi) of Candle Cranberry can be eaten (Bindon and Walley, 1992).

Family Ericaceae Juss.

Casuarina Mistletoe

Botanical Name *Lysiana casuarinae* (Miq.) Tiegh.

Noongar Name Nyilla Nyilla (the generic Noongar name for mistletoe) (Coppin, 2008; Daw et al, 2011).

Field Notes Casuarina Mistletoe is a hemi-parasitic climber obtaining at least part of its nutrients from the host plant. It has thin needle-like leaves and yellow tubular flowers (sometimes with red tips) with six small petals at the top of the tube. The flowers appear from February to September (Bunuru to Djilba). The fruits are small, ovular in shape and are red when ripe. Casuarina Mistletoe is only found in Western Australia from Karratha to Esperance and east to Newman, Wiluna and Kalgoorlie (FloraBase, 2018).

Culinary Uses The edible berries (karlburi) have a sweet, sticky pulp and made a good snack food for Noongars (Coppin, 2008; Cribb and Cribb, 1987; Daw et al, 2011).

Family Loranthaceae Juss.

Botanical Name *Centella asiatica* (L.) Urb., also known as *Hydrocotyle asiatica*.

Other Common Names Asiatic Pennywort and Gotu Kola.

Noongar Name Not known.

Field Notes Centella is a creeping, perennial herb with spreading roots that can sprout new plants from the nodes. It only grows to around 40 cm high. It has almost circular leaves and small, pink or purple-red or white, star-shaped flowers that appear from August to December (Djilba to early Birak) or January to April (late Birak to Djeran). It is usually found in winter-wet depressions (FloraBase, 2018). Centella is endemic to the south-west of Western Australia around the coast from Geraldton to Esperance. It is also found in all the eastern states of Australia except Tasmania, in Southeast Asia

Family Apiaceae Lindl.

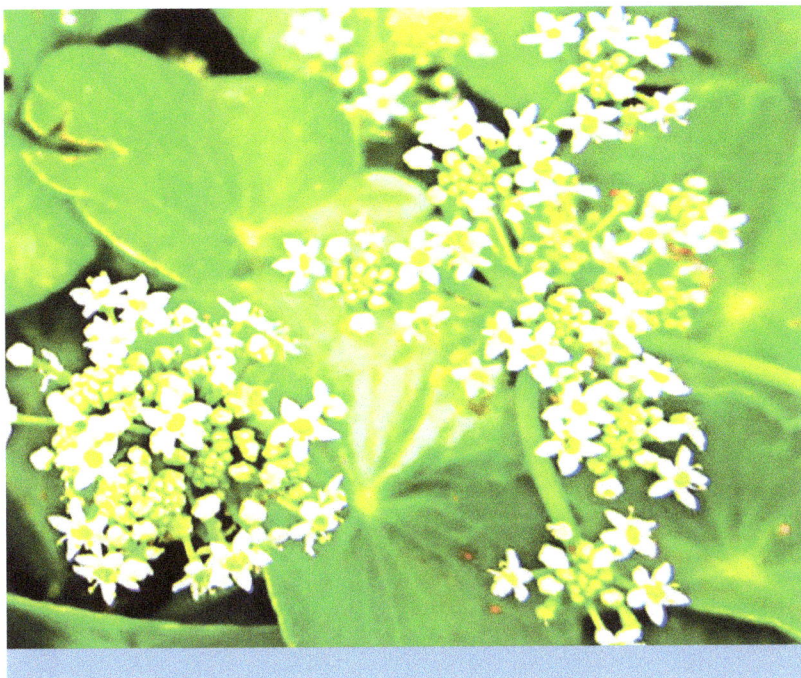

and in some wetland regions of the south-eastern part of the United States of America (EOL, 2018).

Culinary Uses The leaves are edible either raw or steamed (Cribb and Cribb, 1987).

Other Uses Centella is used as a traditional medicine in some Southeast Asian countries, where it is known as Gotu Kola, to treat minor wounds and other conditions such as leprosy, lupus, varicose ulcers, eczema, psoriasis, diarrhoea, fever, amenorrhea, diseases of the female genito-urinary tract, for relieving anxiety and improving cognition (Gohil et al, 2010).

Family Asparagaceae Juss.

Botanical Name *Dichopogon fimbriatus* (R.Br.) J.F.Macbr.

Other Common Name Nodding Chocolate Lily.

Noongar Name Not known.

Field Notes The Chocolate Lily is a small, tuberous, perennial plant growing to around 0.7 m in height. Its thin, green leaves grow to 35 cm long. The orchid-like, purple-pink flowers it produces appear from September to February (late Djilba to early Bunuru). The flowers smell a bit like chocolate, hence the name. In Western Australia, the plant is found all over the south-west (FloraBase, 2018). It is also found in Queensland, Victoria, South Australia and New South Wales (Atlas of Living Australia, 2018).

Culinary Uses The tubers of Chocolate Lily were eaten raw and are reported to be bland and slightly bitter (Coppin, 2008; Low, 1991).

Christmas Tree

Botanical Name *Nuytsia floribunda* (Labill.) G.Don.

Noongar Names Mungai (Bindon and Chadwick, 1992), Mooja (Coppin, 2008; Daw et al, 2011; SERCUL, 2014), Mungah (Meagher, 1975), Moondjak (Whitehurst, 1997) and Moodgar (Perth Region NRM, 2015).

Field Notes The Christmas Tree is so named because it produces spectacular bright yellow flowers around Christmas time; that is, from October to January (Kambarang to late Birak). It grows as a tree or shrub, depending on the conditions, up to 10 m high. Its roots (bwoor) are reported to be parasitic. Its bark (boort) is a rough, grey-brown colour. It is found in a variety of soils on sandplains, slopes and at the base of rocky outcrops in coastal and near-coastal areas from Geraldton to Esperance (FloraBase, 2018).

Family Loranthaceae Juss.

Culinary Uses Hassell (1936) cited in Meagher (1975) wrote:

> *Nuytsia floribunda is a tall tree with deep orange-coloured blossoms. The natives dug up the suckers, which are numerous, peeled off the pale yellow outer bark (boort), and ate the moist brittle centre which tastes like sugar candy.*

Only women (yorgas) were allowed to dig the roots of the Christmas tree. The roots were only eaten in times when food was scarce (Nannup, N., in discussion with the author, July 2018).

Noongars also soaked the flowers in water to make a sweet drink from the nectar (ngonyang) (SERCUL, 2014). Coppin (2008) wrote: 'Slabs of wood were removed to make shields, resulting in raw sweet gum (modyar) to ooze out, later gathered and eaten.' Some Noongar groups don't eat from the tree or pick the flowers because they believe that the tree is where their ancestors rest.

Climbing Lignum

Botanical Name *Muehlenbeckia adpressa* (Labill.) Meisn.

Other Common Name Native Sarsaparilla.

Noongar Name Not known.

Field Notes Climbing Lignum, as the name suggests, is a twining shrub or climber with red stems that can reach up to 2 m in length. Its leaves are up to 6 cm long and 3.5 cm wide. Its small green-yellow, star-shaped flowers appear from September to December (late Djilba to early Birak) (FloraBase, 2018). The plant produces small, green, globular fruits. It is found all over the south-west of Western Australia and around the coast through South Australia, Victoria and southern New South Wales (Atlas of Living Australia, 2018).

Family Polygonaceae Juss.

Culinary Uses The fruits of Climbing Lignum are edible but have a slight sour taste. It is reported that early settlers found the fruit of this plant quite suitable for making fruit pies (Maiden, 1889; Plants for a Future, 2012). Some Aboriginal groups ground the fruit into a pulp and baked the resulting cakes on hot coals (De Angeles, 2005).

Family Capparaceae Juss.

Botanical Name *Capparis spinosa* subsp. *nummularia* (DC.) Fici.

Other Common Names Wild Passionfruit, Moonflower and Caperbush.

Noongar Name Not known.

Field Notes Coastal Caper is a thorny, prostrate, spreading, evergreen shrub that grows up to 2 m in height with branches up to 2 m long. Its leaves are mid-green and ovate with a deep central vein. Its flowers have four white petals and numerous long white stamens. The flower opens at night, as one common name, 'Moonflower', suggests. Its fruit is ovoid, about 4 cm long. Coastal Caper grows along water courses, on open plains, bare ground, depressions and roadsides in

a variety of soils over limestone (Fern, 2018). It is found right across the northern half of Australia. In Western Australia it grows from Kununurra down to the Greater Geraldton area (FloraBase, 2018).

Culinary Uses The fruit is edible when it ripens, that is, when the skin turns orange and splits open and the little black seeds become visible. The seeds are reported to taste hot and spicy. The fruit is sweeter during the warmer months. The young buds, which resemble capers, are also edible (Australian Plants Society, S.A. Inc. 2018; Fern, 2018).

Family Aizoaceae Martinov.

Botanical Names There are two Coastal Pigfaces that are endemic to the south-west of Western Australia. *Carpobrotus virescens* (Haw.) Schwantes and *Carpobrotus rossii* (Haw.) Schwantes.

Other Common Names Bain (*Carpobrotus virescens*) and Karkalla (*Carpobrotus rossii*).

Noongar Names Bain (Coppin, 2008), Kolbolgo, Kolboje and Metjarak (used at Toodjay only) (Abbott, 1983; Moore, 1884b).

Field Notes Coastal Pigfaces are ground-hugging succulent plants with a spread of approximately 3 to 4 m. The purple-pink (and occasionally white) flowers with white bases are around 6 cm in diameter. They appear from June through to January (Makuru to Birak) (Archer, 2017; FloraBase, 2018). The fruit appears after the flowers fall off and are elongated, like the leaves, and purplish-red in colour (SERCUL, 2014).

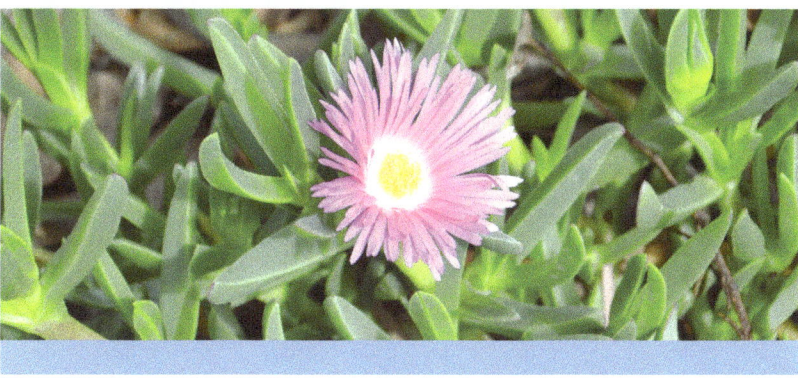

Although there have been sightings of *Carpobrotus rossii* as far north as Canarvon and Shark Bay in Western Australia, it is found mainly along the southern coast from Albany through South Australia and Victoria, and around the Tasmanian coast. *Carpobrotus virescens* is endemic to Western Australia and is found along the coast from Geraldton to Israelite Bay (Atlas of Living Australia, 2018).

Culinary Uses The reddish, edible fruits (majeruk) of the Coastal Pigfaces have a juicy white pulp centre and can be eaten fresh or dried. They have been reported to taste like salty strawberries or figs. The leaves are also edible but need to be boiled or steamed and are eaten as greens (Coppin, 2008; Low, 1991; SERCUL, 2014). As a survival tip, Cribb and Cribb (1987) wrote: 'The leaves contain a large amount of water and can sustain life for a while in an emergency'.

Other Uses Infusions (teas) of the leaves (mangara) of the Coastal Pigfaces were used to treat diarrhoea, dysentery and stomach cramps. They were also used as a gargle for sore throats and laryngitis and mild bacterial and fungal infections of the mouth. The juice of the leaves was also used externally to treat a variety of skin conditions, including fungal infections (such as ringworm and thrush), eczema, dermatitis, herpes, cold sores, cracked lips, chafing, skin conditions and allergies. The juice of the leaves was also rubbed into the body for muscular aches and rheumatism, and was also used much like Aloe Vera, for burns, abrasions, open cuts, grazes, mosquito bites and sunburn (Coppin, 2008).

Coastal Saltbush

Family Chenopodiaceae Vent.

Botanical Name *Rhagodia candolleana* Moq.

Other Common Name Seaberry Saltbush.

Noongar Name Not known.

Field Notes Coastal Saltbush grows as either a spreading or an erect shrub up to 5 m in height. It has ovate bright green leaves and small, pale flowers that appear between December and April (Birak to early Djeran). Its fruits are small, ruby-red berries (karlburi) that have a large stone in the middle. As the name suggests, it is a very coastal plant that thrives in sand (FloraBase, 2018). It is found in coastal areas around the southern reaches of Australia from Geraldton to the northern coast of New South Wales. It is also found around the coast in Tasmania (Atlas of Living Australia, 2018).

Culinary Uses The fruits of Coastal Saltbush are edible and are very sweet when ripe. The leaves are also succulent and tender to eat as a green vegetable and are usually eaten boiled or steamed (Coppin, 2008; Low, 1991).

Coast Beard-heath

Family Ericaceae Juss.

Botanical Name *Leucopogon parviflorus* (Andrews) Lindl.

Other Common Names Tassel Bush and White Currants.

Noongar Name Not known.

Field Notes Coast Beard-heath grows as a densely branched shrub or tree to 3 m in height. Its ovate leaves often have curved tips and are up to 29 mm long and 7.5 mm in width. Its small, white, star-shaped flowers have five petals. They appear in clusters from February to March (Bunuru) or from June to October (Makuru to early Kambarang) depending on the conditions. It bears small, globular fruits that are white when ripe. This plant prefers sandy soils, over limestone or granite, on coastal dunes around the southern coast of Australia from Geraldton north of Perth to southern Queensland (Gott, 2010; FloraBase, 2018).

Culinary Uses The small, white fruits of Coast Beard-heath are edible. They have a tough little stone in the middle and are reported to have a mild lemon flavour (City of Charles Sturt, n.d.; Cribb and Cribb, 1987; Coppin, 2008; Gott, 2010; Low, 1991; Maiden, 1889).

Botanical name *Dianella brevicaulis* (Ostenf.)
G.W.Carr & P.F.Horsfall.

Other Common Names Short-stem Flax-lily and
Black-anther Flax-lily.

Noongar Name Not known.

Field Notes Coast Flax-lily is a tufted, perennial plant that
grows to 0.5 m in height. It is the coastal form of the Blue
Flax-lily (*Dianella revoluta*). The plant spreads through
underground tubers. Long, strap-like leaves arise from the
base of the plant and vary in colour from grey to green. Its
blue, star-shaped flowers with six petals appear from October
to December (Kambarang to early Birak). It bears berry-like,
globular fruit that are blue when ripe. This plant is found
in coastal and near-coastal sandy soils right around the
southern coast of Australia from Perth to southern

Family Hemerocallidaceae R.Br.

New South Wales. It is also found in coastal areas of Tasmania (FloraBase, 2018; State Flora, 2013).

Culinary Uses The blue fruits of Coast Flax-lily are edible when ripe (City of Charles Sturt, n.d.; Wildflower Society of WA, n.d.).

Coast Ground Berry

Botanical Name: *Acrotriche cordata* (Labill.) R.Br.

Other Common Name Coastal Blueberry.

Noongar Name Not known.

Field Notes Coast Ground Berry grows as a prostrate or erect shrub up to 0.6 m high and can have a spread of up to 2 m wide. It has small, ovate, thick, light-green leaves. Its green-white, star-shaped flowers have five petals. They appear from July to December (late Makuru to early Birak). Its fruit are small, green-white, globular berries (karlburi). Coast Ground Berry, as the name suggests, loves sand and is found only near the coast from Dongara to eastern Victoria (Cambridge Coast Care, n.d.; FloraBase, 2018).

Family Ericaceae Juss.

Culinary Uses According to Shoebridge (2004)
'all soft fruits of the Epacridaceae Family (accepted name
Ericaceae) are edible and some flowers contain useful
quantities of nectar'.

Botanical Name *Solanum symonii* H.Eichler.

Other Common Name Kangaroo Apple.

Noongar Name Not known.

Field Notes Coast Oondoroo is an erect shrub that grows to around 2 m in height. Its flowers are blue to pale purple appearing from August to November (Djilba to late Kambarang) or from January to March (late Birak to late Bunuru). Its fruit are green berries (karlburi) tinged with purple, egg-shaped and around 2 cm long. In Western Australia Coast Oondoroo occurs on coastal sands and limestone from Geraldton to the South Australian coast (FloraBase, 2018; Apace WA, n.d.a).

Culinary Uses The green berries (karlburi) of Coast Oondoroo can be eaten but are reported to be somewhat bitter (City of Joondalup, 2011).

Family Solanaceae Juss.

Coast Sword-sedge

Family Cyperaceae Juss.

Botanical Name *Lepidosperma gladiatum* Labill.

Other Common Names Sword Sedge and Kerbein.

Noongar Name Kerbein (SERCUL, 2014; Daw et al, 2011).

Field Notes Coast Sword-sedge grows as tufted, grass-like, perennial plants to 1.5 m in height with a spread of approximately 1.5 m. It spreads by means of its rhizomatous roots. Fluffy brown flowers grow on the end of its stalks from November to May (late Kambarang to Djeran) (FloraBase, 2018). Coast Sword-sedge is native to the south-west of Western Australia and is found all along the south coast of Australia from Geraldton to southern New South Wales. It also grows around the coast in Tasmania (Atlas of Living Australia, 2018).

Culinary Uses The white base of the leaves and stems of Coast Sword-sedge are edible and were eaten by Noongars raw or roasted. It is believed that the leaves were more succulent in the wetter areas of the south-west (Coppin, 2008; SERCUL, 2014). The leaves have a mild laxative effect if too many are eaten (Nannup, N., in discussion with the author, July 2018).

Other Uses The leaves of Coast Sword-sedge were dried and split and woven into string and rope for fishing nets (Explore Melville, 2012; Greenskills, n.d.; SERCUL, 2014).

Botanical Name *Templetonia retusa* (Vent.) R.Br.

Other Common Name Cocky's Tongue

Noongar Name Yackal Djarr (City of Joondalup, 2011) and Injid (Wadandi).

Field Notes Cockies Tongues is a shrub with many branches that grows up to 4 m in height. It has large, red or white-yellow, pea-shaped flowers that appear from April to November (Djeran to late Kambarang). It thrives in sand, clay, and gravel and is found on plateaus, coastal cliffs and hillsides (FloraBase, 2018). It is endemic to the coastal regions of the south-west of Western Australia from Shark Bay to the southern reaches of South Australia (Atlas of Living Australia, 2018).

Culinary Uses The flowers of Cockies Tongues are edible. A tea can be made from the crushed seeds. The seeds are best collected when the seed pods are young. (Nannup, N., in discussion with the author, July 2018).

Family Fabaceae Lindl.

Botanical Name *Clematis pubescens* Endl.

Noongar Name Not known.

Field Notes Common Clematis is a strong, woody shrub or climber that has separate male and female plants. It grows to around 5 m high. It has white-cream, star-shaped flowers with four thin petals. The flowers appear from May to November (late Djeran to Kambarang). It grows in a variety of sands and soils in a variety of habitats. It is indigenous to the south-west of Western Australia and is found in coastal and near coastal areas from Cervantes to Israelite Bay (FloraBase, 2018).

Family Ranunculaceae Juss.

Culinary Uses Noongars ate the tubers of Common Clematis after roasting them in hot ashes (Barrett and Tay, 2016).

Common Pin Heath

Family Ericaceae Juss.

Botanical Name *Styphelia tenuiflora* Lindl.

Noongar Name Gunalpa (Nannup, N., in discussion with the author, July 2018).

Field Notes Common Pin Heath grows as a small, erect shrub up to 1.5 m in height. It has prickly, green, lanceolate leaves with yellow edges and long white-cream flowers up to 30 mm long that appear from March to July (late Bunuru to Makuru). Green, spherical berries (karlburi) appear after flowering. Common Pin Heath thrives in gravelly lateritic soils. It is indigenous to the south-west of Western Australia and is only found there in an area from Cervantes to Albany (FloraBase, 2018).

Culinary Uses The small green berries (karlburi) of Common Pin Heath are edible when ripe (Coppin, 2008).

Daw et al (2011) relate that 'Noongars would chew the succulent coating then spit out the seed where it would grow again'.

Family Haloragaceae R.Br.

Botanical Name *Myriophyllum crispatum* Orchard.

Noongar Name Not known.

Field Notes Common Water Milfoil is an aquatic, annual herb that grows to approximately 60 cm high. It has needle-like, green leaves and small cream or red flowers that are present from October to December (Kambarang to early Birak) or January to February (late Birak to early Buburu). Common Water Milfoil prefers clay soils, mud or black sand and is found in creeks and swamps in the south-west of Western Australia from Perth to Denmark (FloraBase, 2018). It is also found in all the eastern states of Australia including Tasmania (Atlas of Living Australia, 2018).

Culinary Uses The young shoots and leaves of Common Water Milfoil are edible (Oz Watergardens, 2018).

Cottony Saltbush

Family Chenopodiaceae Vent.

Botanical Name *Chenopodium curvispicatum* Paul G.Wilson.

Other Common Name White Goosefoot.

Noongar Name Not known.

Field Notes Cottony Saltbush is a weak, intricately branched, spreading shrub, that grows to around 1 m in height. Its light-green to silvery-grey leaves are a rounded triangular shape. Its flowers are drooping panicles approximately 5 cm long. These are followed by the appearance of red, succulent berries. Cottony Saltbush grows in calcareous loam or sand over limestone or clayey sand over laterite soils in the drier parts of the south-west of Western Australia and other southern states of mainland Australia (Atlas of Living Australia, 2018; FloraBase, 2018; Seeds of South Australia, 2018).

Culinary Uses The berries (karlburi) of this shrub are edible when ripe and bright red (Williams and Sides, 2008).

Botanical Name *Astroloma prostratum* R.Br.

Other Common Names Native Cranberry and Candle Cranberry.

Noongar Name Not known.

Field Notes Cranberry Heath grows as a prostrate or small erect shrub to 0.3 m high. It has prickly leaves with spines down the side and tiny, bright red, candle-shaped flowers that can appear any time from January to November (late Birak to Kambarang). After flowering, small green fruits appear. Cranberry Heath grows in a variety of soils on sandplains, rocky slopes, granite outcrops and hilly areas. This plant is only found near the coast in the south-west of Western Australia from Perth to Esperance (FloraBase, 2018).

Family Ericaceae Juss.

Culinary Uses The small green fruits of Cranberry Heath are edible. They have sweet pulp surrounding a small stone (Cribb and Cribb, 1987; De Angeles, 2005; Maiden, 1889). Botanist Joseph Maiden (1889) cited by Low (1991) wrote, 'Fruits of these dwarf shrubs are much appreciated by the school boys and Aboriginals.'

Desert Kurrajong

Botanical Name *Brachychiton gregorii* F.Muell.

Noongar Name Not known.

Field Notes Desert Kurrajong grows as a tree to 12 m in height. It has evergreen leaves which are often shed in drier periods. The leaves have three or five lobes and are up to 20 cm long. Its flowers are pale-yellow and bell-shaped with reddish margins. They appear from November to January (late Kambarang through Birak). In Western Australia it is usually found growing in sand or sandy loam on undulating sand dunes, rocky ridges or slopes from Exmouth down through the Geraldon Sandplains and Avon Wheatbelt and out east past Kalgoorlie (FloraBase, 2018). It is also found in the Northern Territory and South Australia (Atlas of Living Australia, 2018).

Family Malvaceae Juss.

Culinary Uses The seeds of Desert Kurrajong are edible and were probably ground into flour to make cakes that were baked in hot ashes (Australian Plants Society, S.A. Inc., 2018).

Family Lauraceae Juss.

Botanical Names There are several Dodder Laurels that are endemic to the south-west of Western Australia: *Cassytha flava* Nees, *Cassytha glabella* R.Br., *Cassytha melantha* R.Br., *Cassytha pomiformis* Nees and *Cassytha racemosa* Nees

Other Common Names Devils Twines, Tangled Dodder Laurel, and Large Dodder Laurel.

Noongar Names Not known.

Field Notes Dodder Laurels are leafless, climbing plants that lack roots and bark. They are parasitic vines that climb all over other plants they form around. Their light-green stems are leafless and have no bark as such. The fruits of this species are oval-shaped globules that are almost transparent when they ripen. Dodder Laurels tolerate salt well and only require a good host plant (NQ Dry Tropics, 2015). They

are found covering plants that like winter-wet areas. All the Dodder Laurels listed above are native to the south-west of Western Australia and are mainly found in coastal areas from Geraldton to Esperance (FloraBase, 2018).

Culinary Uses The fruits of Dodder Laurels are edible and were a great snack food for the Noongars, but they are reported to be not very tasty (Coppin, 2008; Cribb and Cribb, 1987; Low, 1991). Daw et al (2011) warn that, because the fruit of the Dodder Laurels contain 'small quantities of a poisonous alkaloid', they should not be eaten in large quantities as this could prove fatal.

Other Uses Small quantities of the fruit can be eaten as a laxative. The juice of the fruit can be applied to cuts and sores to aid the healing process. The vines were used to fashion fishing nets.

Family Orchidaceae Juss.

Botanical Name *Diuris* spp.

Noongar Name Cara or Djubak (Nyungar Wardan Katitjin Bidi – Derbal Nara, n.d.).

Field Notes There are approximately sixty species of Donkey Orchids, over thirty of which are only found in Western Australia (Encyclopaedia Britannica, 2018; Western Australia's Wildflower Country, 2018). They are easily recognised by their bright yellow or yellow and purple flowers with their cute faces and two large petals sticking up at the rear that look like donkey ears. Donkey Orchids are tuberous perennials that only grow to approximately 15 cm or so tall. They have long, thin, green leaves arising from the base of the plants. Their flowers appear in spring (late Djilba to Kambarang) (FloraBase, 2018). Donkey Orchids occur in all

Australian states, except for the Northern Territory (Western Australia's Wildflower Country, 2018).

Culinary Uses Coppin (2008) reports that Donkey Orchid tubers were an important source of food for Indigenous Australians and were eaten either raw or roasted in hot ashes. The tubers are reported to be high in starch, juicy and taste like potatoes (Explore Melville, 2012).

Botanical Name *Lemna disperma* Hegelm.

Noongar Name Not known.

Field Notes Duckweed is a monoecious, free-floating, aquatic, annual, herb. It has clover-like leaves and minute, white flowers that appear from October to December (Kambarang to early Birak). It is found in still, freshwater in coastal habitats from Perth to Esperance (FloraBase, 2018). It is also found in South Australia, southern Queensland, New South Wales, Victoria and Tasmania (Atlas of Living Australia, 2018).

Culinary Uses The leaves are edible raw or steamed (Oz Watergardens, 2018).

Family Araceae Juss.

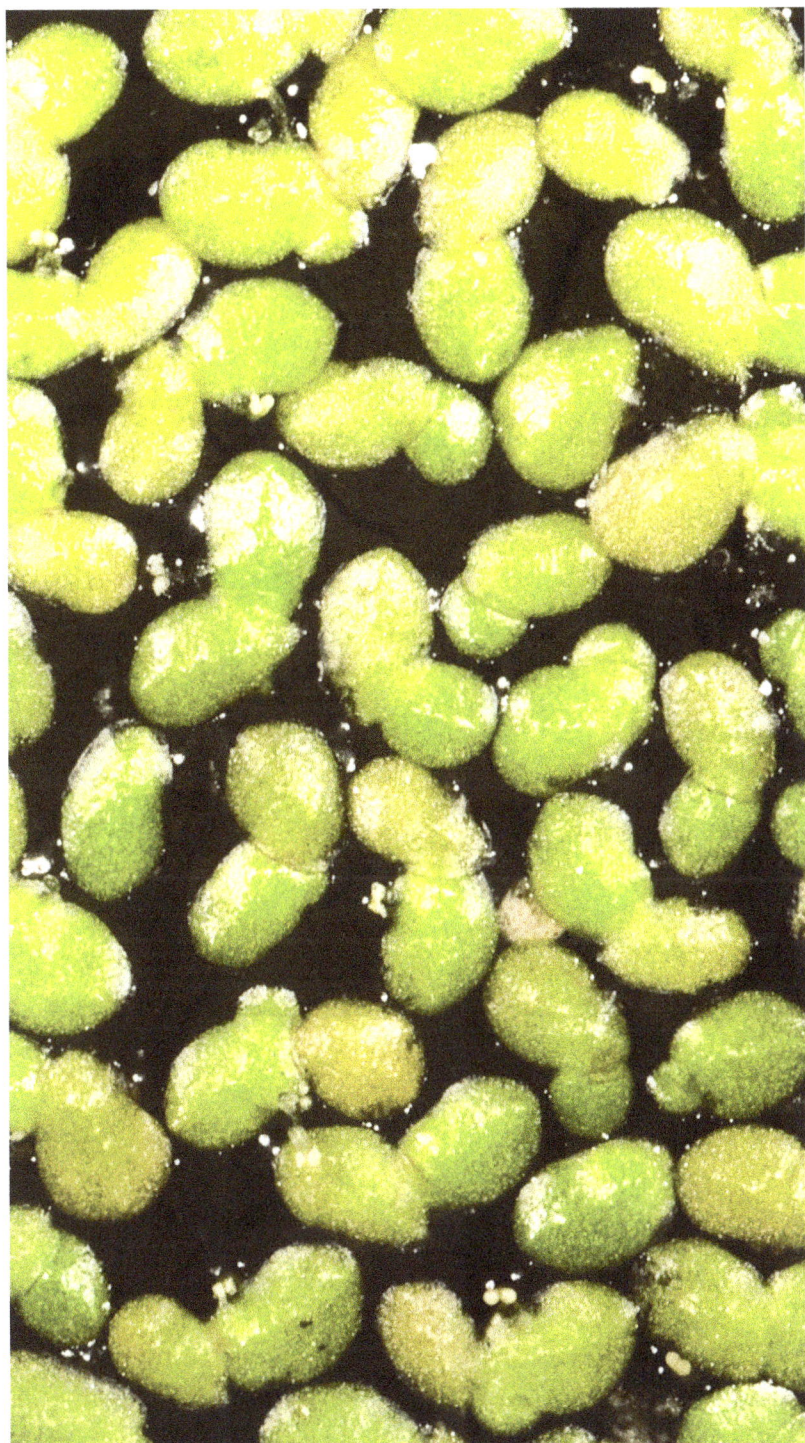

Family Apocynaceae Juss.

Botanical Name *Cynanchum floribundum* R.Br.

Other Common Names Native Pear and Desert Pear.

Noongar Name Not known.

Field Notes Dumara Bush is an erect or scrambling to twining shrub that can grow to around 2 m in height. Its mid-green leaves are ovate to lanceolate and approximately 115 mm long. Its white-cream, star-shaped flowers have five petals and long white stamens. They are present from March to October (late Buburu to early Kambarang). Its fruit are pear shaped and green initially, turning pale yellow as they age (FloraBase, 2018; Flora NT, 2018). Dumara Bush grows in sandy soils along drainage lines, coastal dunes and among granite rocks. It is native to Western Australia where it is found from the Geraldton Sandplains to the far north coast (FloraBase, 2018).

It is also found in the Northern Territory, South Australia and Queensland (Atlas of Living Australia, 2018).

Culinary Uses The whole fruit is edible including the outer case, inner white pith and seeds (Dann, 2003; Welch, 2017).

Dwarf Burchardia

Botanical Name *Burchardia multiflora* Lindl.

Other Common Names Milkmaids and Multi-headed Milkmaids.

Noongar Name Cara (Perth NRM, 2016).

Field Notes Dwarf Burchardia is a tuberous, perennial, herb that grows to approximately 0.3 m in height. It has long, green leaves and pink-white flowers with six petals that appear from July to October (late Makuru to early Kambarang). The petals have pink stripes down the middle. Dwarf Burchardia prefers sand or clay soils around swamps and streams and on granite outcrops. This plant is only found in the south-west of Western Australia between Cervantes and Albany (FloraBase, 2018).

Family Colchicaceae DC.

Culinary Uses The roots and tubers of this plant were a plentiful food source for the Noongars. They were usually roasted in hot ashes before being eaten (Perth NRM, 2016).

Botanical Name: *Wurmbea dioica* (R.Br.) F.Muell.

Noongar Name Not known.

Field Notes Early Nancy is a small plant growing to around 30 cm in height. It has two or three long, thin, grassy, green leaves that arise from the base of the plant. The plant has a small underground corm or bulbotuber. Its white flowers are very attractive. They have six petals with a narrow purple band across each petal, which form a circle near the centre of the flower. Early Nancy starts flowering in winter, hence its common name. The flowers are seen from July to October (late Makuru to early Kambarang) (Oz Native Plants, 2018). In Western Australia the plant can be seen along the coast and inland from Geraldton to Albany (FloraBase, 2018). Early Nancy is found in all other Australian states except the Northern Territory (Atlas of Living Australia, 2018).

Family Colchicaceae DC.

Culinary Uses The small underground corm or bulbotuber of Early Nancy is quite starchy and was reportedly eaten by Indigenous Australians including Noongars. The corms were probably roasted in hot ashes before being eaten (Coppin, 2008; Cribb and Cribb, 1987; Low, 1991).

Eucalypts

There are over 800 species of Eucalypts or Gum Trees of the Myrtaceae family in Australia, a large proportion of which are only found in the south-west of Western Australia. Eucalypts come in all shapes and sizes from small bushes to giant trees. Their leaves, bark, seed capsules (gumnuts) and flowers are also varied. One thing they have in common is that their flowers don't have petals but rather large, colourful stamens which are full of nectar (ngonyang) (Euclid, 2018). Some of the more useful Eucalypts of the south-west of Western Australia are listed in the table.

Common Name	Botanical Name	Noongar Names	Distribution
Blackbutt	*Eucalyptus todtiana* F.Muell.	Dwutta, Maynee (Cunningham, 2005) and Mori (Bindon and Chadwick, 1992)	From Geraldton to Perth and east to the Avon Wheatbelt
Bullich	*Eucalyptus megacarpa* F.Muell.	Bullich (Abbott, 1983)	From Perth to Albany
Caesia	*Eucalyptus caesia* Benth.	Caesia	Avon Wheatbelt and Western Malee
Flooded Gum	*Eucalyptus rudis* Endl.	Kulurda (Wheatbelt NRM, 2015) and Gulurto (Moore, 1884a)	From Geraldton to Bremer Bay

Family Myrtaceae Juss.

Common Name	Botanical Name	Noongar Names	Distribution
Gimlet	*Eucalyptus salubris* F.Muell.	Nardarak, Gnardarup and Ngarrip (Wheat-belt NRM, 2009)	From the Eastern Murchison to Esperance and east past Kalgoorlie
Illyarrie	*Eucalyptus erythrocorys* F.Muell.	Illyarrie	From Kalbarri to Cervantes and around Perth parks and gardens
Jarrah	*Eucalyptus marginata* Sm.	Jarrah, Cherring, Chiaragl, Djara, Djarrail, Djarryl, Djerral,Dyerral, Gharrahel, Jarrail, Jarral, Jeerilya, Jeril, Jerrail, Jerral, Jerryl and Yarrah (City of Joondalup, n.d.)	Around Cervantes and from Perth to Bremer Bay
Karri	*Eucalyptus diversicolor* F.Muell.	Karri and Karril (Abbott, 1983)	From Busselton to Albany
Marri	*Corymbia calophylla* (Lindl.) K.D.Hill & L.A.S.Johnson	Marri, Mari, Marril, Marree, Mundup, Nandup, Nundup, Kurrden, Kardan Cardau, Gardan Grydan (City of Joondalup, n.d.), Mahree, Ngora and Ngumbat (Abbott, 1983)	From Geraldton to Albany and east to the Avon Wheatbelt
Moort	*Eucalyptus platypus* Hook.	Moort and Maalok (Abbott, 1983)	Around Gnowangerup, Jerramungup, and Ravensthorpe

Common Name	Botanical Name	Noongar Names	Distribution
Mottlecah	*Eucalyptus macrocarpa* Hook.	Mottlecar (Abbott, 1983)	From Geraldton to Perth and east to Bruce Rock, Coorow and Quairading
Red-flowering Gum	*Corymbia ficifolia* (F.Muell.) K.D.Hill & L.A.S.Johnson	Boorn and Yorgam	Around Denmark and Albany
Red Heart Gum	*Eucalyptus decipiens* Endl.	Moit (Bennett, 1991)	From Jurien Bay to Albany
Red Morrel	*Eucalyptus longicornis* (F.Muell.) Maiden	Morryl, Poot and Put (Abbott, 1983)	From the Avon Wheatbelt to Esperance and east past Kalgoorlie
River Red Gum	*Eucalyptus camaldulensis* Dehnh.	Gyrdan and Kardan (Bindon and Chadwick, 1992)	Widely distributed, occurring in every mainland state along waterways
Salmon Gum	*Eucalyptus salmonophloia* F.Muell.	Warak, Woonert (Wheatbelt NRM, 2009), Worrick, Wurukk (Bindon and Chadwick, 1992) and Weerluk (Abbott, 1983)	From the Geraldton Sandplains to Albany and Esperance and east past Kalgoorlie

Common Name	Botanical Name	Noongar Names	Distribution
Tallerack	*Eucalyptus pleurocarpa* Schauer	Tallerack (French, 2012)	Around Albany, Dandaragan, Gnowangerup, Jerramungup, Kondinin and Lake Grace
Tuart	*Eucalyptus gomphocephala* DC.	Morrol, Duart, Mooarn, Moorun, Mouarn, Tuart and Tooart (City of Joondalup, 2011; Abbott, 1983)	From Geraldton to Cape Naturaliste
Wandoo	*Eucalyptus wandoo* Blakely.	Wornt, Dooto, Wando, Wandoo and Warrnt (Abbott, 1983)	From Jurien Bay to Albany and Bremer Bay
Yate	*Eucalyptus cornuta* Labill.	Mo, Yandil, Yate and Yeit (Abbott, 1983)	From Busselton to Bremer Bay and Esperance
York Gum	*Eucalyptus loxophleba* Benth.	Daarwet, Doatta, Goatta, Twotta, Wolung, Yandee (Abbott, 1983), Yorgum and Wurak (Bindon and Chadwick, 1992)	From Shark Bay to Esperance and out past Kalgoorlie

Culinary Uses Noongars used Eucalypts to full advantage. Nectar (ngonyang) was extracted either by sucking it directly from the flowers or by soaking the flowers in water to make a sweet drink (Australian Geographic, n.d.; City of Joondalup, 2011). Some eucalypts delivered extra food. For example, the sweet and juicy outer part of the small roots (bwoor) of the Yate, York Gum and Wandoo trees was scraped off and eaten (Coppin, 2008). The seeds of the Marri are edible (Australian Native Nursery, n.d.). The red gum that oozes from the trunk of Yate and Marri trees (mnkar) is edible (Meagher, 1975). The leaves of some Eucalypts, such as the Flooded Gum, are sometimes covered with manna (kulurda), a product of a small mite that lives at the base of the leaves. Noongars used to lick the sugary substance off the leaves or collect it and form it into a large sweet to suck on (City of Joondalup, 2011).

Other Uses Eucalypts also had medicinal properties. The leaves were crushed and used as an antibacterial poultice for healing wounds. Crushed leaves were also held under the nose to relieve nasal congestion due to colds and influenza. The gum (kino) from some Eucalypts was ground and used as an ointment on sores (City of Joondalup, 2011). The gum of all Eucalypts can be eaten to relieve dysentery. The leaves of all Eucalypts in the south-west were also used as bedding and in steam pits for people with colds, influenza and rheumatism. Decoctions (teas) made from the bark (boort) of the River Red Gum were used as a wash for sores, wounds and skin conditions (Hansen and Horsfall, 2016).

(top) Flooded Gum (*Eucalyptus rudis* ssp. *rudis*)
(right) Wandoo Beard Orchid (*Calochilus stramenicola*)
(far right) Mottlecah (*Eucalyptus macrocarpa*)

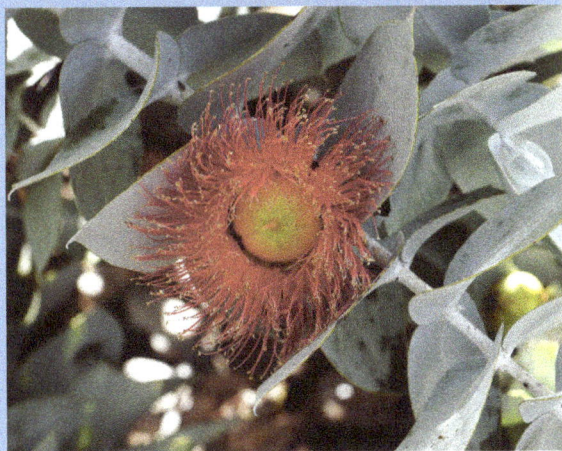

Fringed Leek Orchid

Family Orchidaceae Juss.

Botanical Name *Prasophyllum fimbria* Rchb.f.

Noongar Names Djubak and Tuboc (Meagher, 1975).

Field Notes The Fringed Leek Orchid is an impressive, tuberous, perennial plant that grows to around 1 m in height. The stems can vary between green to almost black in colour. The flowers have white, frilly edges with a light-purple centre. They can appear as early as June but are more commonly seen from August to October (Djilba to early Kambarang). This orchid grows in a variety of soils and is usually found in coastal, winter-wet depressions from Geraldton to Esperance (FloraBase, 2018).

Culinary Uses Moore (1884b) cited in Meagher (1975) wrote of the Fringed Leek Orchid: 'Djubak – An orchis (sic),

the root (bwoor) of which is the size and shape of a new potato and is eaten by the natives. It is in season in the month of October.'

Botanical Name *Thysanotus manglesianus* Kunth.

Other Common Name Climbing Fringe Lily.

Noongar Name Adjiko and Tjunguri, which is the same name Noongars use for a similar plant called Twining Fringe Lily (*Thysanotus patersonii*) discussed on page 356 of this book.

Field Notes The Fringed Lily is a twining, leafless, perennial plant with tuberous roots and stems that can grow to 2 m in length. Beautiful, fringed, purple flowers appear at the end of the stems from August to November (Djilba and Kambarang). This plant only grows in Western Australia from Shark Bay to Esperance. It has also been sighted to the east out past Newman and Kalgoorlie (FloraBase, 2018).

Family Asparagaceae Juss.

Culinary Uses Noongars either ate the watery tuberous roots (bwoor) of the Fringed Lily raw, steamed in an earth oven or baked in hot ashes (City of Joondalup, 2011). Coppin (2008) believes that Noongars ate the stems as well after rolling them in hot ashes and grinding them into a powder, which was then eaten with Eucalypt gum (kino), the same as Tjunguri stems (Twining Fringe Lily - *Thysanotus patersonii*).

Family Asparagaceae Juss.

Botanical Name *Thysanotus thyrsoideus* Baker.

Noongar Name Adjiko (Nannup, N., in discussion with the author, July 2018).

Field Notes The Fringe Lily is a perennial plant that grows to around 35 cm high. It has tuberous roots (bwoor) and purple flowers with fringed petals. The flowers appear from September to November (late Djilba to Kambarang). The Fringe Lily is a native of Western Australia. It grows in a variety of soils and habitats all over the south-west corner from Geraldton to Albany (FloraBase, 2018).

Culinary Uses Noongars ate the tubers of Fringe Lily after roasting them in hot ashes (Barrett and Tay, 2016).

Family Fabaceae Lindl.

Botanical Name *Glycine tabacina* (Labill.) Benth.

Noongar Name Not known.

Field Notes Glycine Pea grows as a prostrate, perennial creeper that either trails along the ground or twines around bushes or trees. Its stems are slender and elongated. Its ovate leaves arise off the stem in clusters of three. Its purple to mauve, pea-shaped flowers appear from September to May (late Djilba to Djeran) (Greening Australia, n.d.). This plant is indigenous to Western Australia but grows more prolifically in the eastern states. In Western Australia this plant grows along the coast and inland from Shark Bay to Busselton (FloraBase, 2018).

Culinary Uses The taproot of the Glycine Pea is edible and is reported to have the flavour of liquorice (Cribb and Cribb, 1987). The taproot was probably eaten after it was roasted in hot ashes.

Golden Kelp

Botanical Name *Ecklonia radiata* (C.Agardh) J.Agardh.

Other Common Name Common Kelp.

Noongar Name Not known.

Field Notes Golden Kelp is a golden-brown, marine, subtidal alga that grows to approximately 2 m in height. Its stalks end in leathery blades that have a smooth, corrugate, or spinous surface. In Australia it is found in shallow water right around the southern coast from Kalbarri to Caloundra in Southern Queensland. It is also found around the Canary Islands, the Cape Verde Islands, Madagascar, Mauritania, Senegal, South Africa, Oman, Lord Howe Island, and New Zealand (iNaturalist, n.d.).

Culinary Uses Golden Kelp is edible and can be eaten fresh or dried for later use (Milkwood, 2016).

Family Lessoniaceae Setch. & N.L. Gardner.

Graceful Grass Tree

Botanical Name *Xanthorrhoea gracilis* Endl.

Noongar Name Mimidi (Daw et al, 2011; Coppin, 2009) and Burarup (Abbott, 1983).

Field Notes The Graceful Grass Tree is a tufted, perennial grass tree with no trunk. The grassy tuft can reach 2 m in height. Its white to cream flowers appear on a spike that can be up to 1.5 m high from October to January (Kambarang to Birak). This plant only grows along the Western Australian coast in sand or sandy loam from Dongara to Albany (FloraBase, 2018).

Culinary Uses Noongars soaked flowers of Mimidi (and other grass trees) in water to make a sweet drink from the nectar (ngonyang) (Coppin, 2008). They also pulled the base of the flower stalk out and ate the juicy pulp on the inside of the base (Daw et al, 2011; Explore Melville, 2012).

Family Xanthorrhoeaceae Dumort.

Granite Pink

Botanical Name *Tribonanthes purpurea* T.Macfarlane & Hopper.

Noongar Name Not known.

Field Notes Granite Pink is a tuberous, perennial herb that grows to around 0.04 m high. Its thin leaves grow to 4 cm in length. Its pink-purple, tubular flowers are around 1 cm long. They appear in the spring (late Djilba to Kambarang). Granite Pink is found in seasonally wet soils in moss among granite rock inland from Perth to Esperance (Florabase, 2018).

Culinary Uses The tubers of Granite Pink are edible and were eaten raw or roasted in hot ashes (Bindon and Walley, 1992).

Family Haemodoraceae R.Br.

Grasses (Gilba, Djiraly and Bobo)

Noongar Generic Names for Grass Bobo, Djirap, Djiraly (Whitehurst, 1997) and Gilba (Bindon and Chadwick, 1992).

Noongar Name for Grain Kwolak (Whitehurst, 1997). The individual names of the grasses are not known.

The seeds of some Australian grasses were a good source of nutrition for Indigenous Australians. They are a good source of starch and contain protein and vitamins. The species of Australian grasses that have edible seeds include *Themeda* spp., *Panicum* spp., *Eragrostis* spp. *and Microlaena* spp.

Opposite is Tindale's (1974) map of the areas that supported grain-producing grasses for Indigenous Australians before colonisation.

Grasses that were cultivated by Aboriginal groups include the following species.

Common Name	Botanical Name	Distribution
Brown's Lovegrass	*Eragrostis brownii* (Kunth) Nees	Perth to Albany
Button Grass	*Dactyloctenium radulans* (R.Br.) P.Beauv.	Kalumburu to Perth
Canegrass	*Eragrostis australasica* (Steud.) C.E.Hubb.	Carnarvon to Perth

Family Poaceae Barnhart & Barnh.

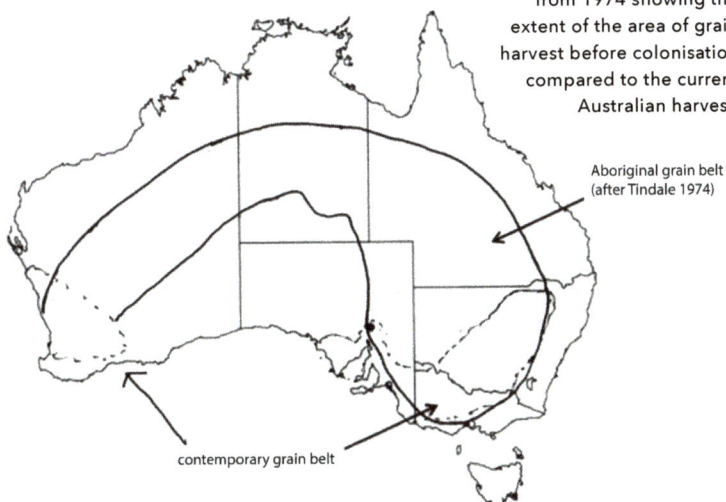

Norman Tindale's map from 1974 showing the extent of the area of grain harvest before colonisation compared to the current Australian harvest.

Aboriginal grain belt (after Tindale 1974)

contemporary grain belt

Common Name	Botanical Name	Distribution
Clustered Lovegrass	*Eragrostis elongata* (Willd.) J.Jacq.	Karratha to Albany
Common Wallaby-grass	*Rytidosperma caespitosum* (Gaudich.) Connor & Edgar.	Shark Bay to the South Australian border
Kangaroo Grass	*Themeda triandra* Forssk.	Most parts of Western Australia
Mallee Lovegrass	*Eragrostis dielsii* Pilg.	Most parts of Western Australia
Native Millet	*Panicum decompositum* R.Br.	Around and to the north of Geraldton
Weeping Grass	*Microlaena stipoides* (Labill.) R.Br.	Kalbarri to Bremer Bay and around Esperance
Windmill Grass	*Chloris truncata* R.Br.	All over the south-west

Culinary Uses Aboriginal groups cultivated and collected the seeds of these grasses and ground them to make flour that was then mixed with water to make damper (mereny), a bush tucker bread they baked in hot ashes or later, after colonisation, in Dutch ovens. (Coppin, 2008; Cribb and Cribb, 1974). Pascoe (2014) has produced evidence, gleaned from the journals of early explorers and settlers, that in some areas of Australia Indigenous Australians were cultivating grain crops, storing the surplus and making bread for millennia before settlement by Europeans and probably before the Egyptians.

Traditionally, damper was made from the flour from ground seeds that was mixed with water to make a dough that was then baked in the ashes of a dying fire. Settlers modified traditional recipes by using plain flour, adding butter, baking powder (or using self-raising flour), and milk or beer instead of water.

If you would like to try to make a damper at home, opposite is a recipe that has been modified for home use.

Other Uses In some parts of Australia Aboriginals made string from the leaves and stems of some grasses to make bags and fishing nets (Australian National Botanic Gardens, 2012; De Angeles, 2005).

Ingredients

450g (3 cups) self-raising (or plain flour with 3 teaspoons of baking powder)

A pinch of salt

80g butter, chilled, cubed

185ml (3/4 cup) water or milk

Method

Preheat your oven to 200°C. Combine the flour and salt in a large bowl. Using fingertips, rub the butter into the flour.

Add the water to the flour mixture, mixing it until the mixture just comes together, adding a little extra water if the mixture is a little dry.

Turn the dough onto a lightly floured surface and knead gently for 1–2 minutes or until smooth. Shape into an 18 cm disc and place on a baking tray that has been greased or covered with baking paper. Dust the damper with a little extra flour and bake in preheated oven for 30 minutes or until the damper is cooked through and sounds hollow when tapped on the base. Serve warm or at room temperature.

Alternatively, if you are out in the bush and have made a campfire, the damper can be baked directly in the coals as the fire dies, or in a Dutch (camp) oven covered with hot coals.

Botanical Name *Xanthorrhoea preissii* Endl.

Noongar Names Balga, Baaluk, Balgarr, Ballak, Balligar, Balluk, Baluk, Barar, Barlock, Barro, Beara, Paaluk and Paluk (Abbott, 1983); Yimmen (Griffiths, 2009), Bor, Borl (Wheatbelt NRM, 2015), Balag (Goode et al, 2015) and Borak.

Field Notes The Grass Tree is a perennial monocot that can grow to 3 m in height. The thin, grass-like leaves that sprout from the top of the plant can grow to 2.5 m in length. The white-cream flowers are produced on a long stalk (waljarp) from June to December (Makuru to early Birak). They protrude like spears from the top of the plant. The flowers turn brown after they have been on the tree for a while (Friends of the Queens Park Bushland, 2011). Grass Trees occur throughout the south-west of Western Australia on the coastal plain near watercourses from Geraldton to Bremer Bay (FloraBase, 2018).

Family Xanthorrhoeaceae Dumort.

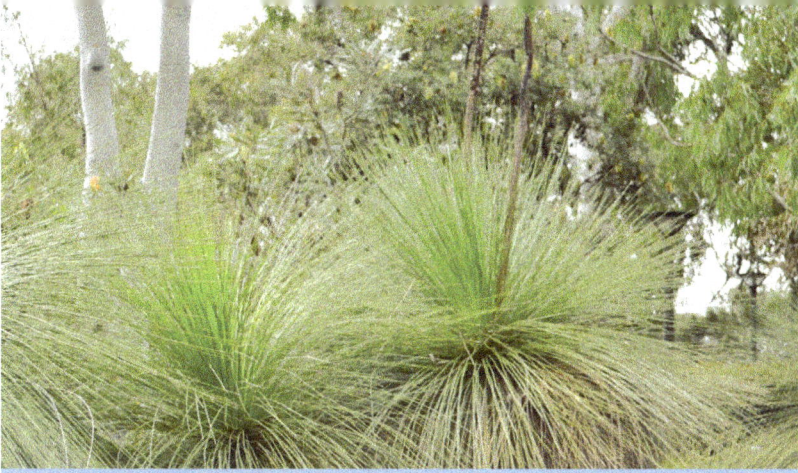

Culinary Uses Noongars soaked the nectar-laden flowers of the Grass Tree in water to make a sweet drink. Gum from flower spikes (mirlen, kadjo, pining or peenck) was used to make cakes (Coppin, 2008; Cribb and Cribb, 1987). Noongars also ate the tender white portion at the base of the leaves (mindar) (Low, 1991). They also ate the Bardi Grubs they collected from dying Balga trees, either raw or lightly roasted in hot ashes (Coppin, 2008; Daw et al, 2011).

Other Uses Parts of the Balga have medicinal properties. The resin or gum (nargalya, nallang, tudibi and biriny) was chewed to relieve both diarrhoea and constipation. The pulp from the inside of the top of the tree was eaten to relieve an upset stomach. Smoke from burning the resin was inhaled to relieve sinusitis (City of Joondalup, 2011). The resin was also used as a binding agent. The resin was first crushed in a heated stone pot with charcoal and kangaroo droppings. The molten resin was used like a cement to bind objects together, such as stone spearheads onto wooden spear shafts. Grass Tree resin was also used as a tanning agent. Lumps of resin were dissolved in water in a rock hole heated by hot stones, then the hides of kangaroo (yonga) and possum (koomal) were scraped and softened and then placed in the rock hole to soak in the tannin mixture. The skins were worn as clothes (bookha), blankets (wogga) or used as a carry-bag (coorda) (City of Joondalup, 2011).

Botanical Name *Grevillea crithmifolia* R.Br.

Noongar Name Berrung (a generic Noongar name for a low, flowering shrub) (City of Joondalup, 2011).

Field Notes Green Carpet, as the name suggests, is a spreading, prostrate shrub that only grows to about 0.6-2 m in height. This plant has beautiful white, spikey flowers that are spread right over the plant from June to November (Makuru to Kambarang). Green Carpet is endemic to Western Australia and is found in sandy soils along the south-west coast from Dongara to Busselton (FloraBase, 2018).

Culinary Uses Green Carpet was an important source of nectar (ngonyang) for Noongars. They either sucked the nectar directly from the flower or made a sweet drink by soaking the flowers in water (City of Joondalup, 2011).

Family Proteaceae Juss.

Family Chenopodiaceae Vent.

Botanical Name *Atriplex cinerea* Poir.

Other Common Name Coastal Saltbush.

Noongar Name Not known.

Field Notes Grey Saltbush grows as an erect or spreading shrub to 1.5 m high. It has light green, ovate leaves and cream or purple, fluffy flowers that appear from September to December (late Djilba to early Birak). Grey Saltbush prefers sandy soil in coastal areas and can be found along the south-west coast from Shark Bay to Israelite Bay (FloraBase, 2018).

Culinary Uses The leaves of the Grey Saltbush can be boiled or steamed and eaten as a vegetable (Coppin, 2008; Cribb and Cribb, 1987; Maiden, 1889).

Hakeas

There are 149 species of Hakea that are endemic to Australia and nearby islands, a good number of which only grow in the south-west of Western Australia. Hakeas are named after Baron Christian Ludwig von Hake, an 18th-century German patron of botany. The flowers of most Hakeas are quite spectacular, and some fruit, like on the Cricket Ball Hakea, have interesting shapes. Some Hakea grow as prostrate shrubs while others grow as erect shrubs to 2 m in height. Flowering times vary throughout the year (Australian Plants Online, 2018). Hakeas were a popular bush tucker plant for Noongars because most of their flowers were laden with nectar (ngonyang). Berrung is a generic Noongar name for a low, flowering shrub (City of Joondalup, 2011). Opposite are some of the more common Hakeas that are endemic to the south-west of Western Australia.

Pincushion Hakea (*Hakea laurina*)

Common Name	Botanical Name	Noongar Name	Distribution
Cricket Ball Hakea	*Hakea platysperma* Hook.	Not known	Geraldton to Yilgarn and east to Coolgardie
Djarnokmurd	*Hakea recurva* Meisn.	Djarnokmurd (Abbott, 1983)	From Geraldton through the Avon Wheatbelt and east to Wiluna
Dungyn	*Hakea oleifolia* (Sm.) R.Br.	Dungyn (Abbott, 1989)	Cape Naturaliste to Bremer Bay
Harsh Hakea	*Hakea prostrata* R.Br.	Berrung, Pulgur, Doolgur (City of Joondalup, 2011) and Janda (SERCUL, 2014)	Geraldton to Esperance
Honey Bush	*Hakea lissocarpha* R.Br.	Djanda (Wheatbelt NRM, 2016)	Geraldton to Esperance
Kangaroo Bush	*Hakea scoparia* Meisn.	Djanja (Wheatbelt NRM, 2016)	Geraldton to Israelite Bay
Myrtle Hakea	*Hakea myrtoides* Meisn.	Not known	Swan Coastal Plain and Avon Wheatbelt
Needle Tree	*Hakea preissii* Meisn.	Tanjinn (Abbott, 1983)	Shark Bay to Esperance and east to Newman, Wiluna and Kalgoorlie
Pincushion Hakea	*Hakea laurina* R.Br.	Kodjet (Abbott, 1983)	Albany to Israelite Bay
Red Pokers	*Hakea bucculenta* C.A.Gardner.	Not known	Shark Bay to Gin Gin

Common Name	Botanical Name	Noongar Name	Distribution
Sea Urchin Hakea	*Hakea petiolaris* Meisn.	Not known	Kalamunda to Lake Grace
Sweet-scented Hakea	*Hakea drupacea* (C.F.Gaertn.) Roem. & Schult, previously known as *Hakea suaveolens*	Not known	Kalamunda to Lake Grace
Two-leaf Hakea	*Hakea trifurcate* (Sm.) R.Br.	Dulgar and Tulga (Moore, 1884b)	Kalbarri to Israelite Bay
Variable-leaved Hakea	*Hakea varia* R.Br.	Not known	Jurien Bay to Esperance
Wavy-leaved Hakea	*Hakea undulata* R.Br.	Not known	Gingin to Albany

Culinary Uses Hakeas were a good source of nectar (ngonyang) for Noongars. As with Banksias and Grevilleas, they either sucked the nectar directly from the flower or made a sweet drink by soaking the flowers in water. They sometimes let the liquid ferment into an alcoholic beverage they called gep (Australian Native Nursery, n.d.; City of Joondalup, 2011). Noongars also roasted the woody fruits of Harsh Hakea in hot ashes and then ate the seeds, which are said to taste like roasted almonds (SERCUL, 2014). Moore (1884b), cited in City of Joondalup (2011), observed that the gum (dolgar, dulgar or tulga) from some Hakeas was eaten by Noongars. It was apparently stored in cakes and carried from place to place as they moved around.

Harsh Hakea *(Hakea prostrata)*

Kangaroo Bush (*Hakea scoparia*)

Red Pokers (*Hakea bucculenta*)

Honeysuckle Grevillea

Botanical Name *Grevillea juncifolia* Hook.

Other Common Names Rush-leaved Grevillea and Spider Flower.

Noongar Names Moncart and Paarluc.

Field Notes Honeysuckle Grevillea is an evergreen shrub or tree that grows from 4 to 7 m in height depending on the conditions. The grey leaves are long and thin with fine hairs on the surface. Its bright, yellow-orange, spider-like flowers are seen at various times of the year, in January (late Birak), from March to May (late Bunuru to Djeran) or from July to November (late Makuru to Kambarang) (Australian Native Plants Society, 2016). Honeysuckle Grevillea is found in rocky, stony and gravelly soil and sand among low trees and in shrubland (Australian Native Plants Society, 2018). Honeysuckle Grevillea is indigenous to the drier areas of all

Family Proteaceae Juss.

Australian states except Victoria and Tasmania (Atlas of Living Australia, 2018). In the south-west, it is found in the drier areas from Geraldton to Perth and has been seen beyond Newman, Wiluna and Kalgoorlie (FloraBase, 2018). Because of its beautiful flowers, it is a prominent feature in parks and gardens around Perth.

Culinary Uses Noongars and other Indigenous groups either sucked the nectar (ngonyang) directly from the flowers of the Grevilleas or soaked them in water to produce a sweet drink. Sometimes the drink was allowed to ferment to produce an alcoholic beverage called gep (City of Joondalup, 2011).

Other Uses The bark of the Honeysuckle Grevillea was burned, and the ash rubbed on sores and wounds, either as is or chewed, to encourage healing (Peile, 1997).

Botanical Name *Carpobrotus modestus* S.T.Blake.

Noongar Name Bayiny (Whitehurst, 1997).

Field Notes Inland Pigface is a prostrate, perennial, succulent plant, similar in looks to Coastal Pigface (*Carpobrotus virescens*). Its trailing stems can grow to around 50 cm in length and they often root at the nodes. Its blue-green leaves are generally around 3 to 7 cm in length but are sometimes tinged pink. As with the coastal variety, the leaves have sharp edges rather than being rounded. Its light purple flowers are approximately 2 cm in diameter when open. The flowers are present from August to November (Djilba and Kambarang). The fruits are fleshy, oblong to ellipsoid in shape, purplish in colour and from 1.5 to 2 cm in length. Inland Pigface, as the name suggests, is found inland, but coastal pockets of the plant exist. Its distribution in

Family Aizoaceae Martinov

Western Australia ranges from Geraldton to Israelite Bay. It is also found in South Australia, Victoria, New South Wales and Southern Queensland (FloraBase, 2018; Victorian Resources Online, 2015).

Culinary Uses The fleshy fruit of Inland Pigface and the leaves are edible and were eaten fresh or dried (Daw et al, 2011; Kapitany, 2015).

Jointed Rush

Botanical Name *Baumea articulata* (R.Br.) S.T.Blake.

Noongar Names Waargyl Ngarnak ('Waargyl's Beard', named after the Waargyl) and Kuiarch (Perth Region NRM, n.d.a).

Field Notes Jointed Rush is a rhizomatous, perennial, grass-like sedge that grows to around 2.6 m in height. Its pendulous, red to brown flowers can appear all year, but mainly from Sepember to December (late Djilba to early Birak). It prefers wet sands and waterlogged soils around swamps and on the border of lakes. Jointed Rush is indigenous to the south-west of Western Australia and is found in coastal and near coastal areas from Geraldton to Esperance (FloraBase, 2018). It is also found around the coast in all eastern states of Australia as far north as Cairns.

Family Cyperaceae Juss.

Culinary Uses Like some of the other sedges the rhizomatous roots (bwoor) of Jointed Rush are edible. Noongars ate them after roasting them in hot ashes (Perth Region NRM, n.d.b).

Other Uses Noongars hollowed out the inside of the Jointed Rush stems and used them as a snorkel when hunting ducks (yerderap) from under the water (Perth Region NRM, n.d.c).

Botanical Name *Pterostylis recurva* Benth.

Noongar Name Kara and Kararr (City of Joondalup, 2011).

Field Notes The Jug Orchid is a tuberous, perennial plant that grows to around 0.8 m in height. It is easily recognised by its prominent green and white jug-shaped flowers, which appear, usually four to a plant, from August to October (Djilba to early Kambarang). This orchid is only found in the south-west corner of Western Australia from Cervantes to Israelite Bay (FloraBase, 2018).

Culinary Uses Noongars ate the edible tubers of the Jug Orchid, which are high in starch and taste somewhat like a potato. They were eaten either raw or roasted in hot ashes (City of Joondalup, 2011; Explore Melville, 2012).

Family Orchidaceae Juss.

Kangaroo Paws and Cats Paws

There are eleven species (and thirteen recognised sub-species) in the genus *Anigozanthos*. The closely related Black Kangaroo Paw (*Macropidia fulginosa*) belongs to the same family and is similar in form. Kangaroo Paws are closely related to the Bloodroots discussed earlier in the book. Kangaroo Paws vary in height from the small Dwarf Kangaroo Paw (*Anigozanthos gabrielae*), which only grows to 20 cm, to the Tall Kangaroo Paw (*Anigozanthos flavidus*) which has been found up to 3 m high. They all have linear, strap-like leaves and tubular flowers that look like little animal paws, hence the names. In the wild the flower colours range from red and green through various shades of reds, greens and yellows to the black and green of *Macropidia fuliginosa*. Several hybrids have been created and there is now a white kangaroo paw. The flowers are present in the Western Australian wildflower season (August to November or Djilba to Kambarang) (ANBG, 2018). The Mangles or Red and Green Kangaroo Paw is the Western Australian state floral emblem.

The most common species of Kangaroo Paw that grow in Noongar country are listed in the table.

Common Name	Botanical Name	Noongar Name	Distribution
Albany Catspaw	*Anigozanthos preissii* Endl.	Not known	Denmark to Albany
Black Kangaroo Paw	*Macropidia fuliginosa* (Hook.) Druce.	Nollamara	Dongara to Perth
Branched Catspaw	*Anigozanthos onycis* A.S. George.	Not known	Around Albany, Jerramungup, Plantagenet and Ravensthorpe
Catspaw	*Anigozanthos humilis* Lindl.	Kurulbrang (City of Joondalup, 2011)	Geraldton to Esperance
Dwarf Kangaroo Paw	*Anigozanthos gabrielae* Domin.	Not known	Albany region
Green Kangaroo Paw or Swamp Kangaroo Paw	*Anigozanthos viridis* Endl.	Koroylbardany (Perth Region NRM, n.d.b) and Koroylbardang (Abbott, 1991)	Perth to Denmark
Little Kangaroo Paw	*Anigozanthos bicolor* Endl.	Not known	Gin Gin to Albany and around Esperance
Mangles Kangaroo Paw or Red and Green Kangaroo Paw	*Anigozanthos manglesii* D.Don.	Kurulbrang (Perth Region NRM, 2015), Nollamara, Yonga Marra (City of Joondalup, 2011) and Knulbora	Shark Bay to Albany
Red Kangaroo Paw	*Anigozanthos rufus* Labill.	Not known	Albany to Israelite Bay
Tall Kangaroo Paw or Evergreen Kangaroo Paw	*Anigozanthos flavidus* DC.	Not known	Busselton to Albany
Yellow Kangaroo Paw	*Anigozanthos pulcherrimus* Hook.	Not known	Dongara to Perth

Culinary Uses Noongars ate the rhizomatous roots (bwoor) either raw or roasted in hot ashes (City of Joondalup, 2011; Plants of the World Online, 2018). Sometimes the roots were ground into a paste, which was then formed into cakes and baked in hot ashes.

Albany Catspaw (*Anigozanthos preissii*)

Catspaw (*Anigozanthos humilis*)

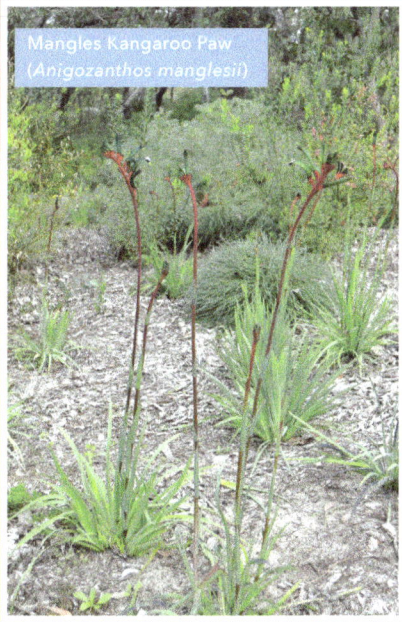

Red Kangaroo Paw
(*Anigozanthos rufus*)

Mangles Kangaroo Paw
(*Anigozanthos manglesii*)

Family Apiaceae Lindl.

Botanical Name *Platysace cirrosa* Bunge.

Other Common Name Native Potato (also applicable to other species of *Platysace*).

Noongar Name Kanna (Abbott, 1983) and Karna.

Field Notes Karna is a twining or climbing, perennial plant with a round tuberous rootstock. Its small, star-shaped, yellow flowers appear from January to March (late Birak to Bunuru). Karna is endemic to and only found in the south-west of Western Australia in coastal and near-coastal lateritic and loamy soils from Geraldton to Bunbury (FloraBase, 2018).

Culinary Uses Karna was another good source of starch for Noongars who ate the tubers either raw or roasted in hot ashes (NACC, n.d.).

Botanical Name *Platysace maxwellii* (F.Muell.) C.Norman.

Other Common Name Native Potato (also applicable to other species of *Platysace*).

Noongar Names Karno (Meagher, 1975), Kukine (Archer, 2017), Koon (Whitehurst, 1997) and Kona (SWALSC, 2016).

Field Notes Karno is an erect or straggling, tuberous shrub growing to 1.2 m in height. It has very thin, lanceolate leaves and small, star-shaped, white flowers with five petals that appear from October to April (Kambarang to early Djeran) (FloraBase, 2018). Karno has a symbiotic relationship with the Eucalypt Wandoo (*Eucalyptus wandoo*) and is mostly found around the base of this tree where it taps into the Wandoo's root system (Nannup, N., in discussion with the author, July 2018). Karno is only found in the south-west of

Western Australia in coastal and inland habitats from Geraldton to Esperance (FloraBase, 2018).

Culinary Uses Karno was an important source of food for Noongars (Archer, 2018). The tubers are available throughout the year and were eaten roasted, or sometimes raw to quench the thirst (Meagher, 1975).

Knotted Club Rush

Botanical Name *Ficinia nodosa* (Rottb.) Goetgh., Muasya & D.A.Simpson.

Other Common Name Knobby Club Rush.

Noongar Name Yangjet (Perth Region NRM, n.d.b).

Field Notes Knotted Club Rush is an erect, rhizomatous, perennial sedge that grows in clumps to around 1 m in height. Its brown to cream flowers appear from October to January (Kambarang to Birak). It prefers sandy soils on coastal dunes and flats around swamps and salt lakes. It is found around the south-west coast from Geraldton to Israelite Bay (FloraBase, 2018). It is alo found around the coast in all the eastern states of Australia as far north as the Sunshine Coast (Atlas of Living Australia, 2018).

Family Cyperaceae Juss.

Culinary Uses As with some other sedges, the roots (bwoor) of the Knotted Club Rush are edible and were probably roasted in hot ashes before eating (Perth Region NRM, n.d.b).

Other Uses The stalks of the Knotted Club Rush were sometimes used to weave nets for catching fish (djildjit) and turtles (yakan) (Perth Region NRM, n.d.b).

Botanical Name *Astroloma serratifolium* (DC.) Druce.

Other Common Name Kick Bush.

Noongar Names Murrumburru (Meagher, 1975), Kondrung and Condrun (Abbott, 1983).

Field Notes Kondrung grows as a prostrate or erect spreading shrub to 1.2 m in height spreading to 2 m wide. Its green, ovate leaves have thorny edges. It produces pink, tubular flowers with red tips that can be present throughout the year. The fruit of the Kondrung is a small green berry. Kondrung is only found in the south-west of Western Australia in coastal and inland habitats from Geraldton to Esperance (FloraBase, 2018).

Family Ericaceae Juss.

Culinary Uses The small green berries (karlburi) of Kondrung were eaten by Noongars as a snack food (Archer, 2017; Meagher, 1975).

Family Cyperaceae Juss.

Botanical Name *Schoenoplectus tabernaemontani* (C.C.Gmel.) Palla, also known as *Schoenoplectus valida*.

Other Common Names Softstem Bulrush, Grey Club-rush, Lake Club-sedge and River Club-rush.

Noongar Name Waargyl Ngarnak (literally Waargyl's Beard) (City of Joondalup, 2011).

Field Notes Lake Club-rush is a robust, rhizomateous, perennial sedge that grows to around 2 m in height. It spreads along underground stems. Its leaves are basal sheaths with blades up to 10 cm long. Its red-brown flowers are pointy spikelets. In Australia they are present from November to April (late Kambarang to early Djeran) (Yarra Ranges, 2010b). This species is found in many countries around the world including most European countries, Australiasia, Africa and the Americas (Encyclopedia of Life,

2018). In the south-west of Western Australia, Lake Club-rush is found from Perth to Albany (FloraBase, 2018). It is also found in all the eastern states including Tasmania (Atlas of Living Australia, 2018).

Culinary Uses The rhizomes of the Lake Club-rush are edible and were eaten by many Indigenous groups around the world (Encyclopedia of Life, 2018).

Other Uses Some Indigenous groups used the stems to weave mats and baskets (Encyclopedia of Life, 2018).

Leafless Ballart

Family Santalaceae R.Br.

Botanical Name *Exocarpos aphyllus* R.Br.

Noongar Names Chuk, Chukk, Dtulya and Merrin (Abbott, 1983).

Field Notes Leafless Ballart is a small, erect tree that grows from 3 to 5 m in height. Its finely furrowed branches sometimes end in a sharp point. The leaves are scale-like and are flattened against the branches (Lassak and McCarthy, 2008). The yellow-green flowers are minute. They appear from April to May (Djeran) or from September to November (late Djilba to Kambarang) or in January (late Birak) depending on the conditions (FloraBase, 2017). The fruits are spherical red berries (karlburi) 4 to 5 mm in diameter (Bindon, 1996). The Leafless Ballart is indigenous to the south-west of Western Australia and is found from Shark Bay

around to the South Australian border (FloraBase, 2018). It is also found in inland Queensland, New South Wales and Victoria (Lassak and McCarthy, 2008).

Culinary Uses The fruits of the Leafless Ballart are edible (Archer, 2018; Cribb and Cribb, 1987). Archer (2018) conveys that:

> Like many other Ballarts the fruits are quite sweet and edible, however the tasty part is not from the developing seed but is the expanded pedicel (flower stalk) developed after the formation of the seed portion that sits atop it. Aborigines regarded these little tasty treats as children's food, being considered not worth the effort of collecting for general consumption.

Other Uses Decoctions (teas) of the mashed stems of the Leafless Ballart were taken internally for colds and applied externally to wash sores and as a poultice on the chest for 'wasting diseases', such as tuberculosis or cancer (Bindon, 1996).

Botanical Name *Lepidium foliosum* Desv.

Noongar Name Not known.

Field Notes Leafy Peppercress is a small shrub that only grows to 60 cm in height. Its stem leaves are triangular or oblanceolate to obovate and grow to around 4 cm long and 10 mm wide. Its small, white flowers appear in May (Djeran). Leafy Peppercress is found in sand over limestone or granite around the south-west coast from Cervantes to Israelite Bay (FloraBase, 2018). It is also found in South Australia, Victoria and Tasmania (Atlas of Living Australia, 2018).

Culinary Uses All plants of the *Lepidium* genus are supposed to have edible leaves and stems and were eaten steamed (Coppin, 2008; Low, 1991).

Family Brassicaceae Burnett.

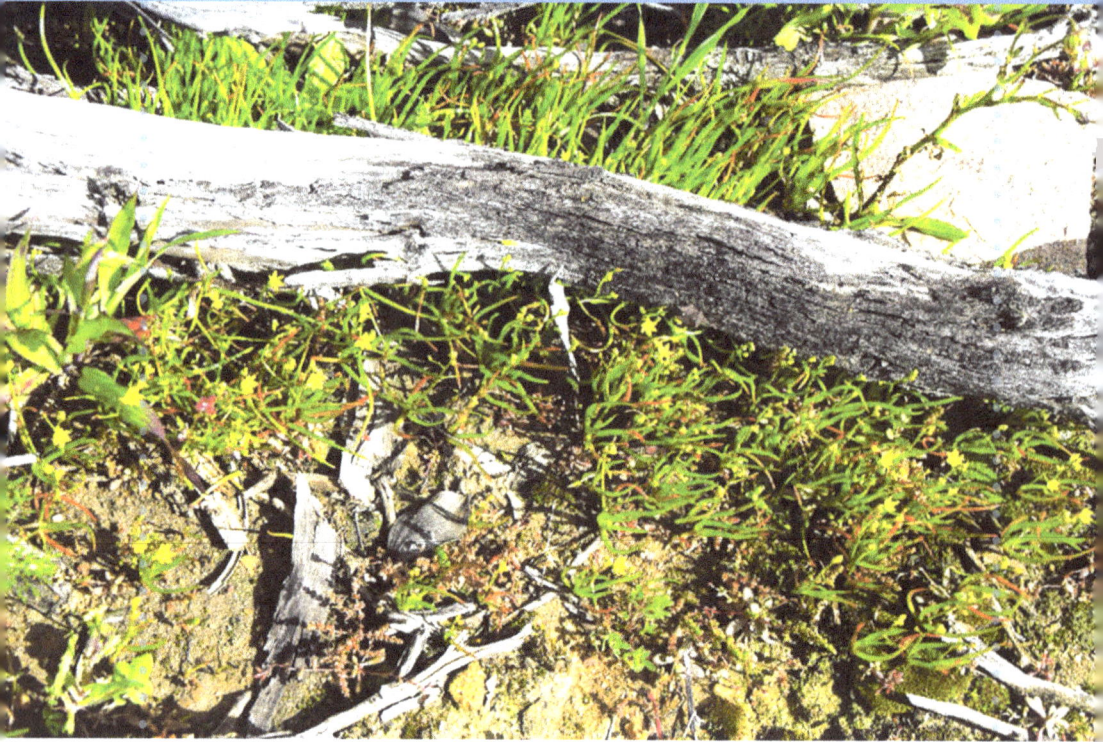

Botanical Name *Bulbine semibarbata* (R.Br.) Haw.

Other Common Names Native Leek or Wild Onion.

Noongar Name Meenar (SWALSC, 2017).

Field Notes Leek Lily is an annual or perennial herb that only grows to around 0.45 m in height. Its green leaves are clustered at the base of the plant and can be up to 27 cm long. Its flowers are yellow and star-shaped with six petals. The flowers can appear any time from July to December (Makuru to early Birak) but are mainly seen from September to October (late Djilba to early Kambarang). Leek Lily is found in most areas of the southern half of Australia and grows quite prolifically in the south-west of Western Australia (Atlas of Living Australia, 2018; FloraBase, 2018).

Family Asphodelaceae Juss.

Culinary Uses The leaves of the Leek Lily can be boiled or steamed and eaten as a green vegetable (Gott, 2010).

Family **Myrtaceae Juss.**

Botanical Name *Callistemon phoeniceus* Lindl.

Other Common Names Scarlet Bottlebrush and Fiery Bottlebrush.

Noongar Name Tubada (Abbott, 1983; Nevill, 2008).

Field Notes The Lesser Bottlebrush grows as a large, bushy shrub to 3 m in height with a spread of about 2 m. Its long, thin, lanceolate leaves are pale green, and its bottlebrush-type flowers are a rich scarlet colour, 10 to 15 cm long, growing at the end of slender branches. The flowers normally appear from November to December (late Kambarang to early Birak) but if the conditions are right it may flower a second time in February (Bunuru) (Australian Nation Botanic Gardens, 2015). This shrub is only found in the south-west

of Western Australia in coastal and inland habitats from Geraldton to Israelite Bay and east as far as Kalgoorlie (FloraBase, 2018).

Culinary Uses The flowers of Bottlebrushes are a good source of nectar (ngonyang) and the Noongars either sucked the nectar straight from the flower or soaked the flowers in water to make a sweet drink (SERCUL, 2014).

Family Polygonaceae Juss.

Botanical Name *Duma florulenta* (Meisn.) T.M.Schust., also known as *Muehlenbeckia florulenta* Meisn.

Other Common Name Tangled Lignum.

Noongar Name Not known.

Field Notes Lignum is a shrub with thin, tangled branches that grows to 3 m in height. Its leaves have a sheath at the base and are are up to 7 cm long, 10 mm wide and are pointed at the end. It has male and female flowers usually on different plants. Its flowers are tiny (less than 3 mm across), cream to pale green, with five petals, growing usually in dense clusters along the stems. The flowers are present throughout most of the year. Lignum grows right across the southern reaches of Australia, but not in Tasmania (Atlas of Living Australia, 2018; PlantNET, 2018).

Culinary Uses The young shoots of Lignum are edible (Williams and Sides, 2008).

Lilac Hibiscus

Botanical Name *Alyogyne huegelii* (Endl.) Fryxell, formerly known as *Hibiscus huegelii*.

Other Common Name Native Hibiscus.

Noongar Name Not known.

Field Notes Lilac Hibiscus grows as a shrub to 4 m in height with a similar spread. It has bright green, hairy leaves with three to five lobes and large, deep purple, white, yellow or pink hibiscus-shaped flowers that can appear from June to January (Makuru to Birak). Lilac Hibiscus is native to the south-west of Western Australia where it tolerates a variety of soils in coastal and near coastal habitats from Shark Bay to Esperance (FloraBase, 2018). It is also found in South Australia (Atlas of Living Australia, 2018).

Family Malvaceae Juss.

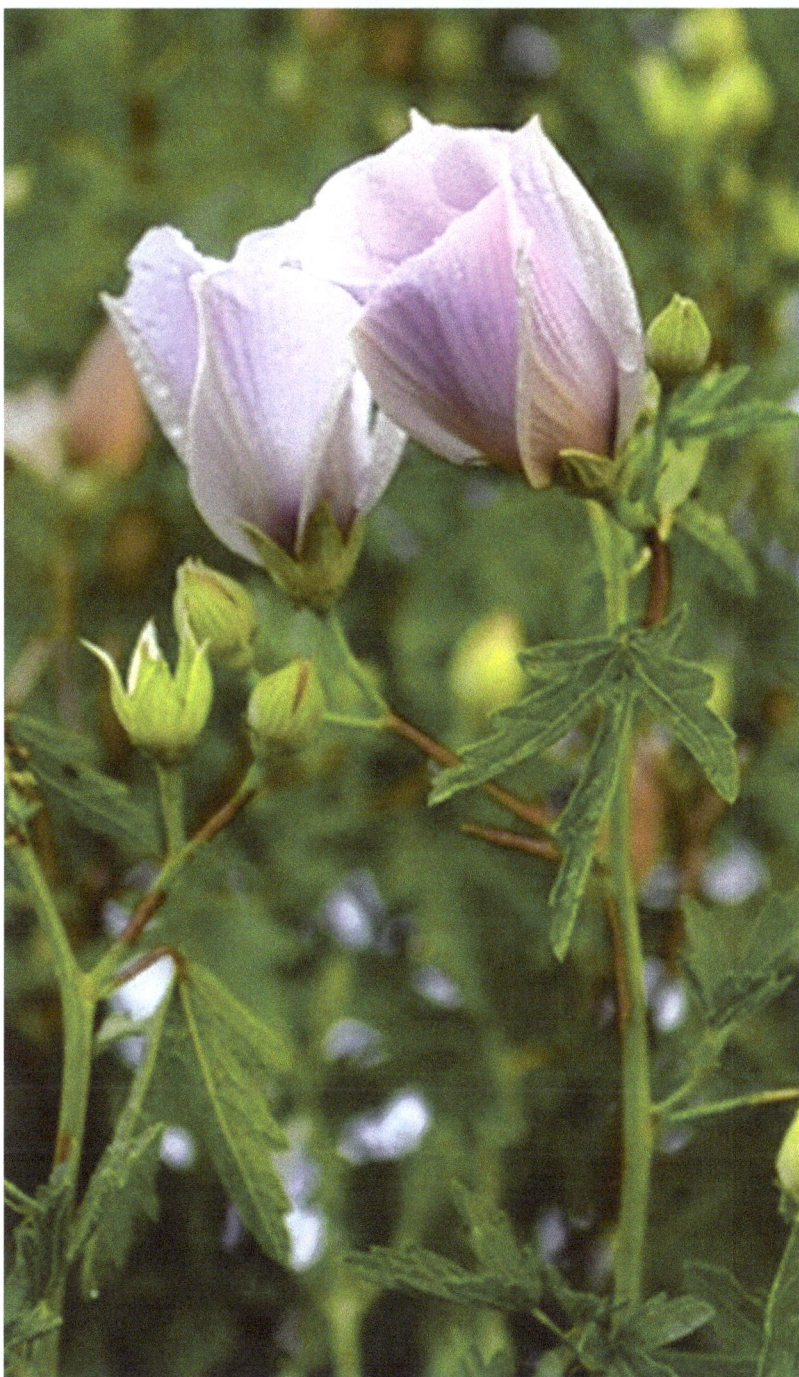

Culinary Uses The flowers, leaves and roots of the Lilac Hibiscus are edible (Australian Plants Society, S.A. Inc., 2018).

Mallee Riceflower

Botanical Name *Pimelea microcephala* R.Br.

Other Common Names Shrubby Riceflower, Small-headed Riceflower and Shrub Kurrajong.

Noongar Name Not known.

Field Notes Mallee Riceflower is a small shrub with many branches that grows from 0.8 to 2.5 m in height. It has separate male and female plants. Its small, greenish-yellow, star-shaped flowers appear in clusters in late winter or early spring (Djilba and Kambarang). Its lanceolate leaves are up to 40 mm long and are in a cluster of four at the base of the flower. The fruit consists of yellow-green or red berries (karlburi) (Bindon, 1996). The plant grows in every state of Australia except Tasmania. It can be found in the inland, drier areas of Noongar territory (FloraBase, 2018).

Family Thymelaeaceae Juss.

Culinary Uses The fruit and the flower of Mallee Riceflower are edible (Bindon, 1996).

Other Uses Decoctions (teas) made by boiling the crushed root of Mallee Riceflower in water were drunk by Aboriginal groups for throat and chest complaints. The bark taken off the roots was effective in reducing pain when wrapped around the head or other parts of the body (Lassak and McCarthy, 2001). The fibre of the inner bark (boort) of this shrub has been used for making string, fishing line and fine mesh nets (Bindon, 1996).

Mallee Saltbush

Botanical Name *Rhagodia preissii* Moq.

Noongar Name Not known.

Field Notes Mallee Saltbush is a shrub that grows to 4 m in height. It has ovate leaves and clusters of green-yellow-white flowers that are present from April to October (Djeran to early Kambarang). After flowering it produces small, red berries. It is found in sand, loam or clay on coastal sand dunes and inland from Karratha to the South Australian / Victorian border (FloraBase, 2018; Atlas of Living Australia, 2018).

Culinary Uses The red berries of the Mallee Saltbush are edible when ripe (Wildflower Society of WA, n.d.).

Family Chenopodiaceae Vent.

Maroon Bush

Botanical Name *Scaevola spinescens* R.Br.

Other Common Names Cancer Bush, Prickly Fanflower and Currant Bush.

Noongar Name Murin Murin (Natural Cancer Treatment, 2012).

Field Notes Maroon Bush is a medium size shrub that grows to around 2 m in height. Its ovate leaves are long and thin. Its fan-like, creamy-white to yellow flowers are present for most of the year. The fruit appears as a small, purplish berry or currant (Crago, n.d.; FloraBase, 2017). Maroon Bush is found in the drier, inland regions of Western Australia as well as Central Australia and New South Wales (Lassak and McCarthy, 2008). It is quite widespread in Western Australia but is only found in the drier outer areas of Noongar country (FloraBase, 2018).

Family Goodeniaceae R.Br.

Culinary Uses The purple berries (karlburi) of Maroon Bush are edible and made a good snack for the Noongars who lived in the drier areas (SERCUL, n.d.).

Other Uses Maroon Bush was a good source of medicine for Noongars. Decoctions (teas) made from boiling the whole plant in water were drunk for cancer, intestinal problems, heart disease, urinary and kidney problems and as an immune system stimulant (Cribb and Cribb, 1983; Lassak and McCarthy, 2008). Decoctions of the stems were taken internally to treat sores and boils. The entire plant was burned and the fumes inhaled to treat colds (Hansen and Horsfall, 2016).

Marsh Club-rush

Botanical Name *Bolboschoenus caldwellii* (V.J.Cook) Sojak.

Noongar Name Belillah (City of Joondalup, 2011).

Field Notes Marsh Club-rush is a rhizomatous, perennial, grass-like plant that grows to around 2 m in height. Its thin, green leaves are approximately 50 cm long and are alternate up the stems. The reddish-brown, fluffy flowers appear at the top of the stems. This plant grows in water around swamps and on river banks between Perth and Busselton (FloraBase, 2018; New South Wales Flora Online, 2018). It is also found in South Australia, Victoria, Tasmania, New South Wales and Southern Queensland (Atlas of Living Australia, 2018).

Culinary Uses The round corms (bulbotubers) of Marsh Club-rush are about the size of walnuts and are edible. Noongars collected them in summer (Birak and early

Bunuru), roasted them in hot ashes and then pounded them with stones. The resulting pulp was then shaped into cakes and baked in hot ashes (City of Joondalup, 2011; De Angeles, 2005; Gott, 2010).

Melaleucas

There are around 300 species of Melaleucas, more commonly known as Paperbarks, Honeymyrtles or Teatrees, although some species of *Leptospermum* are also called Teatree. Some are only small shrubs growing to around 1 m in height, while others can grow up to 100 m high. Their flowers resemble bottlebrushes. Colours of the flowers include white, cream, mauve, pink and red. Melaleucas occur in most parts of Australia and some on off-shore islands and in Papua New Guinea, but there are more species in the south-west of Western Australia than anywhere else.

In the table are some Melaleucas common to the south-west of Western Australia.

Common Name	Botanical Name	Noongar Name	Distribution
Banbar	*Melaleuca teretifolia* Endl.	Banbar	Cervantes to Busselton
Broombush	*Melaleuca hamata* Fielding & Gardner	Kwidjard (Nevill, 2008)	Geraldton to Israelite Bay an east past Kalgoorlie
Broombush	*Melaleuca uncinata* R.Br.	Kwytyart and Yilberra (Abbott, 1983)	Avon Wheatbelt, Eastern Goldfield, Eastern Murchison, Recherche and Western Mallee

Common Name	Botanical Name	Noongar Name	Distribution
Chenille Honeymyrtle	*Melaleuca huegelii* Endl.	Not known	Along the coast from Shark Bay to Cape Naturaliste
Graceful Honeymyrtle	*Melaleuca radula* Lindl.	Moorngan	Geraldton to Perth and east past Kalgoorlie
Granite Bottlebrush	*Melaleuca elliptica* Labill.	Gnow (Bindon and Chadwick, 1992; Hassell, 1975)	Albany to Israelite Bay and north to Kalgoorlie
Greenough Gold Bottlebrush	*Melaleuca megacephala* F.Muell.	Not known	Geraldton to Cervantes
Heart Leaf Honey Myrtle	*Melaleuca cordata* Turcz.	Not known	Geraldton to Esperance and east to Kalgoorlie
Mallee Honey-myrtle	*Melaleuca brevifolia* Turcz.	Not known	Cervantes to Israelite Bay and South Australia
Mindiyed	*Melaleuca nesophila* F.Muell.	Mindiyet (Hassell, 1975)	Esperance to Israelite Bay
Moonah	*Melaleuca preissiana* Schauer.	Moonah	Jurien Bay to Albany
Rottnest Teatree	*Melaleuca lanceolata* Otto.	Moonah (Bennett, 1991)	Shark Bay to the South Australian border and across the southern states into southern Queensland
Rough Honeymyrtle	*Melaleuca scabra* R.Br.	Wurru (Wheatbelt NRM, 2016)	Shark Bay to Esperance

Common Name	Botanical Name	Noongar Name	Distribution
Salt Paperbark	*Melaleuca halmaturorum* Miq.	Not known	Avon Wheatbelt to Esperance and South Australia
Saltwater Paperbark	*Melaleuca cuticularis* Labill.	Bibool (Wheatbelt NRM, 2009), Yaularung, Bewel, Koil and Mudurda (Bindon and Chadwick, 1992)	Perth to Israelite Bay
Scarlet Honeymyrtle	*Melaleuca fulgens* R.Br.	Not known	Dalwallinu, Dowerin, Esperance, Greater Geraldton and Kellerberrin
Swamp Paperbark	*Melaleuca rhaphiophylla* Schauer	Yowarl, Bibool Boorn, Yeymbac, Yiembak (City of Joondalup, 2011) and Yawl (Bindon and Chadwick, 1992)	Geraldton to Esperance

Culinary Uses Melaleucas were a great source of nectar (ngonyang) for Noongars who either sucked the nectar directly from the flowers or soaked the flowers in water to make a sweet drink called mangite or mungitch. Sometimes they fermented the liquid to make an alcoholic beverage called gep (City of Joondalup, 2011).

Other Uses Crushed leaves of some Melaleucas were also used by Noongars, who inhaled the vapours to treat head colds and influenza. The leaves and stems of some Melaleucas were also crushed and heated and applied to the body as poultices for aches and pains. The leaves were also used for smoking ceremonies. The bark can be pulled off some Melaleucas in large sheets and would have been used before colonisation as a clean surface for food, a food and water container and to wrap meat from animals, such as frogs (kweeyar), fish (djildjit) or kangaroo (yonga), before placing it on hot coals or in an earth oven to cook (City of Joondalup, 2011). The paperbark from some Melaleucas was often used for temporary shelters.

Salt Paperbark (*Melaleuca halmaturorum*)

Banbar (*Melaleuca teretifolia*)

Broom Bush (*Melaleuca uncinata*)

Chenille Honeymyrtle
(*Melaleuca huegelii*)

Midget Greenhood Orchid

Botanical Name *Pterostylis mutica* R.Br.

Noongar Name Not known.

Field Notes The Midget Greenhood Orchid is a tuberous, perennial orchid that only grows to around 20 cm in height. Its green leaves arising from the base of the plant form in rosettes and are ovate and up to 3 cm long. It can have up to twenty green flowers at the top of the stem. Each flower has six petals with the top three joined together to form a hood, the bottom two joined together, and a tongue petal or labellum in the middle (New South Wales Flora Online, 2018). The flowers are present from July to October (late Makuru to early Kambarang). The Midget Greenhood Orchid is found growing in a variety of soils on slopes, in claypans, near saline lakes and on winter-wet sites. In Western Australia it is endemic to a triangular area from Coolgardie to Albany and

Family Orchidaceae Juss.

Esperance (FloraBase, 2018). It is also found in Queensland, New South Wales, Victoria, South Australia and Tasmania (Atlas of Living Australia, 2018).

Culinary Uses The tuberous roots of the Midget Greenhood Orchid are edible (Lim, 2016).

Family Colchicaceae DC.

Botanical Name *Burchardia congesta* Lindl.

Noongar Name Kara (Perth Region NRM, 2015; SERCUL, n.d.).

Field Notes Milkmaids are an erect, tuberous, perennial, plant with a single stem that can reach 0.8 m in height. It has grass-like leaves and a spray of cream to white flowers with six petals and yellow centres that appear from August to November (Djilba to Kambarang) (SERCUL, n.d.). Milkmaids are only found in the south-west of Western Australia in coastal habitats from Geraldton to Albany (FloraBase, 2018).

Culinary Uses The starchy corms (tubers) of Milkmaids appear after flowering. They were an important source of food for Noongars who ate them raw or roasted in hot ashes (City of Joondalup, 2011; Cribb and Cribb, 1987; Daw et al, 2011;

De Angeles, 2005; Gott, 2010; SERCUL, n.d.). The tubers are reported to taste like potatoes (Daw et al, 2011).

Family Marsileaceae Mirb.

Botanical Names *Marsilea drummondii* A.Braun. and *Marsilea mutica* Mett.

Noongar Name Ngalkoo (Nannup, N., in discussion with the author, July 2018).

Field Notes There are two Nardoos that are endemic to the south-west of Western Australia: Common Nardoo (*Marsilea drummondii*) and Rainbow Nardoo (*Marsilea mutica*). They are perennial, spreading ferns that spread by underground rhizomes. They are aquatic or semi-aquatic plants that love waterholes, rivers and swamps. They are sometimes found in over a metre of water. Their green leaflets have four sections like a four-leaf clover. Common Nardoo flowers in September (Djilba) whereas Rainbow Nardoo flowers from April to August (Djeran to early Djilba). They reproduce by means of a sporocap (FloraBase, 2017). They are endemic to all

mainland states of Australia. Only Rainbow Nardoo is found in Tasmania (Atlas of Living Australia, 2017).

Culinary Uses All over Australia Indigenous Australians ground the dried sporocaps and removed the husks. The resulting flour was moistened and made into cakes which were baked over coals (Coppin, 2008; Gott, 2010; Low, 1991). According to Chaffey (2002) the sporocarps contain the enzyme thiaminase, which destroys vitamin B1, which could result in the consumer developing Beri-beri. Mixing the sporocap flour with water washes away or dilutes the enzyme, minimising its effect. According to Pascoe (2014) some Indigenous groups also steamed and ate the green tops of the Nardoo plant as a green vegetable. Some Indigenous groups ground the roots into a paste and baked the resulting cakes in hot ashes (De Angeles, 2005).

Botanical Name *Wahlenbergia capillaris* (G. Lodd.) G. Don.

Other Common Names Tufted Bluebell, Common Bluebell and Austral Bluebell.

Noongar Name Not known.

Field Notes The Native Bluebell is a tufted, erect, perennial herb that grows to approximately 6 cm high. Its small, basal, slightly hairy, lanceolate leaves are 50 mm long by 6 mm wide. Its blue, bell-shaped flowers with five petals are present for most of the year. The Native Bluebell prefers sandy, loamy soils or granitic soils and can be found along watercourses, halophytic flats and rocky hillsides all over the south-west of Western Australia from Exmouth to Israelite Bay (FloraBase, 2018; Yarra Ranges, 2009). It is also found

in all other mainland states and territories (Atlas of Living Australia, 2018).

Culinary Uses The flowers of the Native Bluebell are edible and were enjoyed by Aboriginal groups right across mainland Australia. They are a great addition to salads (Sustainable Gardening Australia, 2018; Yarra Ranges, 2009).

Native Cranberry

Botanical Name *Astroloma microcalyx* Sond.

Noongar Name Cadgeegurrup.

Field Notes Native Cranberry is a small shrub with many branches that grows to 100 cm in height with a 50 to 100 cm spread. Its stems are slightly hairy. Its small leaves are 10 mm long by 2 mm wide, are tapered to a point and have hairy edges. The leaves are sometimes curved backwards. Its flowers are bright red tubes approximately 10 mm long and are constricted at both ends. Its flowers are present from June to September (Makuru and Djilba). Its fruits are small berries (karlburi). Native Cranberry can grow in a wide range of soils but needs good drainage (Food Plants International, 2016). Native Cranberry is indigenous to the south-west of Western Australia and is found from Perth to Margaret River (FloraBase, 2018).

Culinary Uses The fruits of Native Cranberry are edible (Food Plants International, 2016).

Family Ericaceae Juss.

Native Geranium

Botanical Name *Geranium solanderi* Carolin.

Other Common Names Native Carrot and Australian Cranesbill.

Noongar Names Kwerdiny (Whitehurst, 1997), Kwordiny (SWALSC, 2016) and Quirting (Hassell, 1975).

Field Notes Native Geranium grows as an erect or prostrate plant to 0.5 m in height. It has a large, red, carrot-like taproot, large green leaves with multiple segments and pink or blue flowers with five petals that appear from August to December (Djilba to early Birak). This plant is found all over the south-west corner of Western Australia from Cervantes to Albany with another pocket near Esperance (FloraBase, 2018). It also grows in South Australia, Victoria, Tasmania, New South Wales and Queensland (Atlas of Living Australia, 2018).

Culinary Uses The starchy, pale red, new season taproots of Native Geranium can be eaten roasted but are reported to have a slightly bitter flavour (Cribb and Cribb, 1987; Low, 1991).

Family Geraniaceae Juss.

Native Hibiscus

Family Malvaceae Juss.

Botanical Name *Alyogyne hakeifolia* (Giord.) Alef., previously known as *Hibiscus hakeifolius*.

Noongar Name Not known.

Field Notes Native Hibiscus grows as an erect or spreading shrub up to 3 m in height. The dark green, needle-like leaves grow to 100 mm in length and 2 mm wide. Its Hibiscus-like flowers can be blue-purple, purple or cream-yellow. They can appear in May (late Djeran) or from August to December (Djilba to early Birak) or from January to February (late Birak to early Bunuru). Native Hibiscus prefers red sandy soils or rocky loam on undulating plains (Australian Native Plants Society (Australia), 2017; FloraBase, 2016). This plant is indigenous to the south-west of Western Australia as well as the southern part of South Australia (Atlas of Living Australia, 2018; FloraBase, 2018).

Culinary Uses The roots (bwoor) of Native Hibiscus are edible. Noongars roasted them in hot ashes before eating them (Australia Native Nursery, n.d.).

Family Scrophulariaceae Juss.

Botanical Name *Myoporum montanum* R.Br.

Other Common Names Water Bush, Boomeralla, Native Daphne and Western Boobialla.

Noongar Name Not known.

Field Notes Native Myrtle grows as a spreading, much-branched shrub or tree up to 4 m in height. It has thin, green, lanceolate leaves and white flowers with purple spots near the centre that appear from May to December (late Djeran to early Birak). The fruit of the Native Myrtle is ovoid in shape and purple when ripe. Only the Noongars around Geraldton would have access to the fruits of this plant as it only grows around Geraldton and to the north in Western Australia (FloraBase, 2018). It is more common in the eastern states of Australia (Atlas of Living Australia, 2018).

Culinary Uses The small, purple fruits of Native Myrtle were a good snack food for Noongars when ripe but, although sweet, are reported to have a salty, bitter edge to them (Coppin, 2008; Cribb and Cribb, 1987; Low, 1991).

Family Plantaginaceae Juss.

Botanical Name *Plantago debilis* R.Br.

Other Common Name Shade Plantain.

Noongar Name Not known.

Field Notes Native Plantain is a ground-hugging herb with a slender taproot. Its dark green, hairy leaves with toothed edges around 6 cm long arise from the base of the plant. Small white flowers appear on one or two stalks from August to December (Djilba to early Birak). Native Plantain is found all over southern Australia including Tasmania (New South Wales Flora Online, 2018). In Western Australia, it is found all over the south-west from Jurien Bay to Esperance and east out beyond Kalgoorlie (FloraBase, 2018).

Culinary Uses In some areas, Indigenous Australians used the bruised seeds of Native Plantain to make a kind of porridge. The leaves are also edible (Low, 1991).

Other Uses When warmed and crushed the leaves yield a sap used to draw swelling from sprains and as poultices on sores such as ulcers, boils and carbuncles (Nyalar Mirungan-ah Nature Refuge, 2013).

Botanical Name *Codonocarpus cotinifolius* (Desf.) F.Muell.

Other Common Names Desert Poplar, Fire Tree, Bell Fruit Tree, Horseradish Tree, Quinine Tree, Medicine Tree, Firebush, Western Poplar and Toothache Tree (Lassak and McCarthy, 2008).

Noongar Name Not known.

Field Notes Native Poplar is a tall shrub or small tree that grows to around 10 m in height. It has pale green, ovate leaves that are tapered at the ends but broader near the tip. The bark has dark red, yellow and green wavy lines. Its bell-shaped fruits are green (Lassak and McCarthy 2008). Yellow-green flowers appear from April to October (Djeran to early Kambarang) (FloraBase, 2018). The Desert Poplar occurs in

Family Gyrostemonaceae A.Juss.

the drier regions of all states of Australia except Tasmania (Atlas of Living Australia, 2018; Lassak and McCarthy, 2008).

Culinary Uses The sappy roots (bwoor) of Native Poplar are edible (Cribb and Cribb, 1987).

Other Uses The roots (bwoor), leaves and shoots of Native Poplar were chewed and used as a narcotic for toothache and general pain relief. Decoctions (teas) of the bark (boort), roots and stems, made by boiling the parts in water, were used externally as an antiseptic wash for skin problems such as eczema and sores and as a rub for rheumatic pain, colds, influenza and fever (Hansen and Horsfall, 2016).

Botanical Name *Tetragonia tetragonoides* (Pall.) Kuntze.

Other Common Names New Zealand Spinach and Warrigal Greens.

Noongar Name Not known.

Field Notes Native Spinach grows as a prostrate plant that can spread to around 2 m. Its leaves are ovate or diamond-shaped and approximately 100 mm long. Its small, yellow flowers appear at the leaf bases and are present for most of the year (Australian Native Plants Society (Australia), 2018). Although this plant is indigenous to Western Australia it is only found around Perth, Denmark and Albany (FloraBase, 2018). It does however grow prolifically in South Australia, Victoria, Tasmania, New South Wales and Southern Queensland (Atlas of Living Australia, 2018).

Family Aizoaceae Martinov.

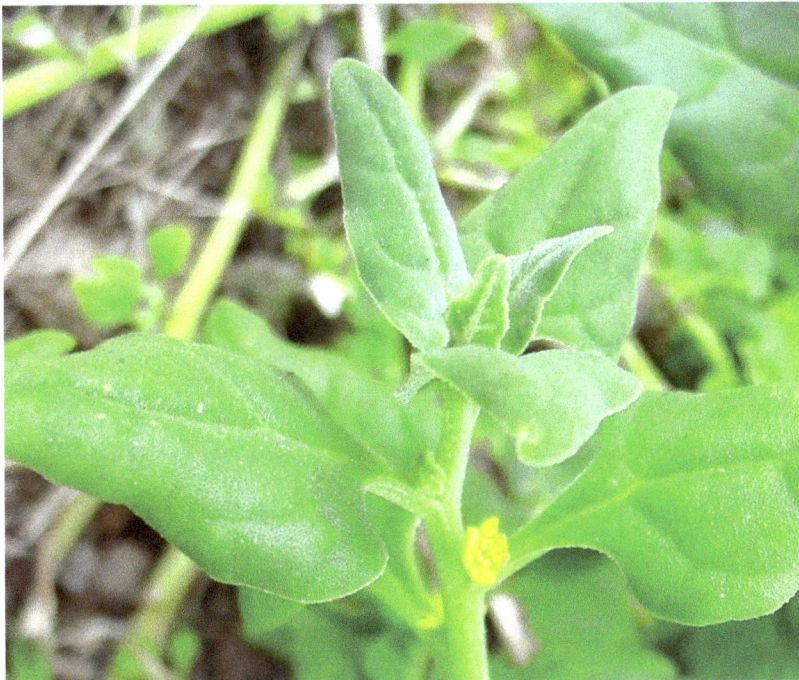

Culinary Uses The leaves of Native Spinach can be eaten raw in a salad or boiled as a green vegetable (Cribb and Cribb, 1974; De Angeles, 2005; Gott, 2010; Isaacs, 1992; Low, 1991; Maiden, 1889). The Australian Native Plants Society (Australia) (2018) warns that 'the leaves contain a high level of oxalic acid which must be leached out by blanching before eating. This can be done by plunging the leaves into boiling water for a minute or so. The water should be discarded'.

Neptune's Necklace

Botanical Name *Hormosira banksii* (Turner) Decne.

Other Common Names Neptune's Pearls, Necklace Seaweed, Sea Grapes, and Bubbleweed.

Noongar Names Nula, Wurlok or Ngoorla (generic Noongar names for seaweed) (Nyungar Wardan Katitjin Bidi – Derbal Nara, n.d.; Bindon and Chadwick, 1992).

Field Notes Neptune's Necklace is a distinctive algae or seaweed made up of strings of dark brown or green, hollow, saltwater-filled, spherical or ovoid beads that are joined together by a short stalk that may be up to 30 cm in length and 15 mm in diameter. It is found near the shore from King George Sound in Western Australia around the southern coast to Port Macquarie in northern New South Wales. It is also found around the coast in New Zealand (Davey, 2000).

Culinary Uses The beads of Neptune's Necklace are edible when young and were usually pierced to get rid of the salt water inside before eating them raw or cooked (Pereira, 2016).

Family Hormosiraceae Fritsch

Nitre Bush

Family Nitrariaceae Lindl.

Botanical Name *Nitraria billardierei* DC., formerly *Nitraria schoberi*.

Other Common Names Dillon Bush, Karumbil and Wild Grape.

Noongar Name Not known.

Field Notes Nitre Bush grows as a spreading, rigid, sometimes spiny shrub up to 2 m in height with a spread of up to 4 m. It has fleshy, long, ovate leaves and small, white, star-shaped flowers that appear from July to December (late Makuru to early Birak). Its grape-like fruits are initially green but turn red when ripe. Nitre Bush is endemic to Western Australia and grows on coastal sandplains from Shark Bay to the South Australian border (FloraBase, 2018). It is also found in all other states except Tasmania (Atlas of Living Australia, 2018).

Culinary Uses The fruits of Nitre Bush are edible when ripe and are reported to taste like salty grapes (Cribb and Cribb, 1974; Gott, 2015; Low, 1991; Maiden, 1889).

Family Asparagaceae Juss.

Botanical Name *Dichopogon preissii* (Endl.) Brittan.

Noongar Name Not known.

Field Notes Nodding Chocolate Lily is a tuberous, perennial plant that grows to around 0.5 m in height. Its purple or pink flowers, one to a stalk, appear from August to October (Djilba to early Kambarang). This plant only grows in the south-west of Western Australia in coastal and near coastal sandy loams from Geraldton to Albany (FloraBase, 2018).

Culinary Uses Noongars ate the tuberous roots of the Nodding Chocolate Lily raw, but the roots are reported to taste a bit bland (Coppin, 2008; Cribb and Cribb, 1987).

Old Man Saltbush

Old Man Saltbush

Botanical Name *Atriplex nummularia* Lindl.

Other Common Names Bluegreen Saltbush, Cabbage Saltbush and Giant Saltbush.

Noongar Names Purngep, Pining (Esperance) and Binga.

Field Notes Old Man Saltbush is a shrub that grows to around 3 m in height and can have up to a 4 m spread. The plant has oval, scaly, silver-grey leaves that usually have serrated edges. Old Man Saltbush has male and female flowers that occur on separate plants. The female flowers form in dense clusters along stems about 20 cm long whereas the male flowers form in disjunct globules at the ends of stems. The flowers appear at different times throughout the year depending on the conditions. (Department of Primary Industry, 2010; Lassak and McCarthy, 2008). Old Man Saltbush is found from the drier regions of

south-west of Western Australia through to South Australia, Victoria, New South Wales and south-western Queensland (FloraBase, 2017; Lassak and McCarthy, 2008).

Culinary Uses Old Man Saltbush seeds can be ground into flour, which is then mixed with water to make damper (mereny). The leaves, when blanched in boiling water, can be used to wrap around meat or fish for cooking purposes. The leaves can be boiled or steamed as a green vegetable, or can be eaten raw in salads (Gott, 2010; SERCUL, 2014).

Other Uses Decoctions (teas) of the leaves, made by boiling the crushed leaves in water for a few minutes, were used externally as a skin cleanser and to bathe skin sores, burns and wounds (Hansen and Horsfall, 2016; Lassak and McCarthy, 2008).

Family Myrtaceae Juss.

Botanical Name *Calothamnus quadrifidus* R.Br.

Noongar Names Kwowdjard and Quietjat (Abbott, 1983; City of Joondalup, 2011).

Field Notes One-sided Bottlebrush grows as either an erect or spreading shrub up to 1 m high. Its long, thin, green leaves are slightly furry. The tree is so named because the red or cream brush-type flowers only have 'bristles' on one side of the stem. The flowers appear from June to December (Makuru to early Birak). This plant is endemic to Western Australia and is found in the south-west corner of the state from Shark Bay to Israelite Bay (Australian Native Plants Society (Australia), 2018; FloraBase, 2018).

Culinary Uses The flowers of this shrub were another good source of nectar (ngonyang) for Noongars, who either extracted the nectar by sucking it directly from the flower or

by soaking them in water to make a sweet drink. Sometimes the resulting sweet liquid was left to ferment into a drink they called gep (City of Joondalup, 2011; SERCUL, 2014).

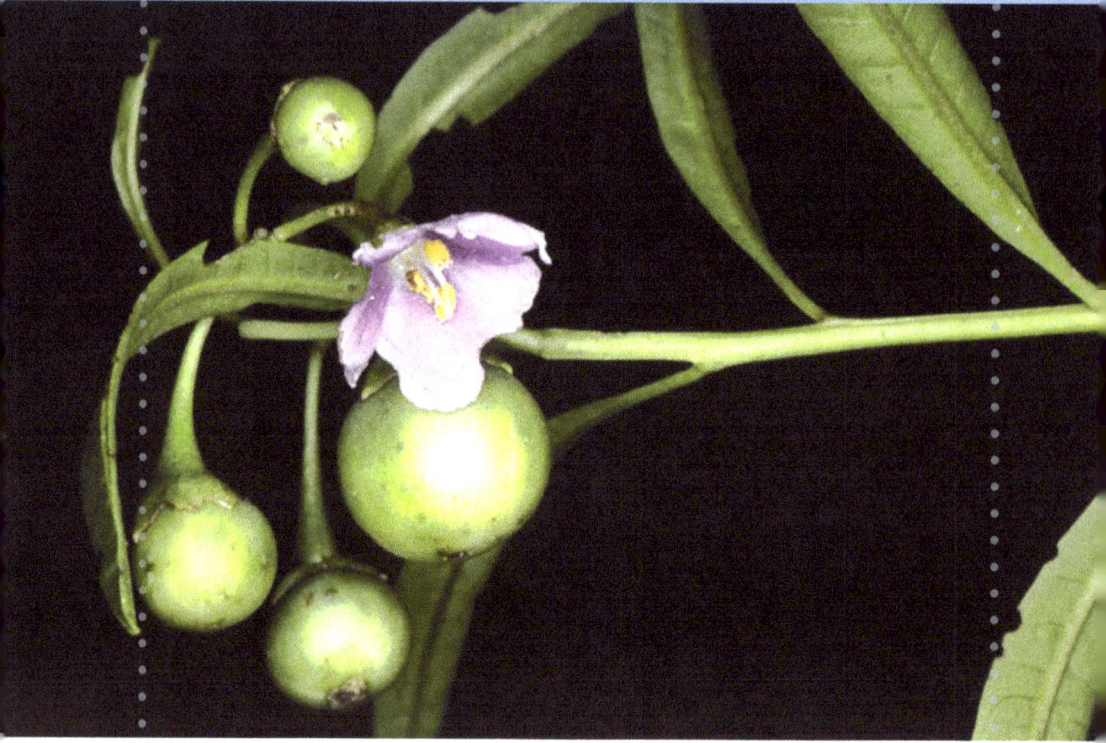

Botanical Name *Solanum simile* F.Muell.

Noongar Name Not known.

Field Notes Oondoroo is an erect shrub that grows up to 2 m in height. It has long, lanceolate, dark green leaves that alternate up the stems. Its round, blue to violet flowers have five lobes. They appear from September to November (late Djilba to Kambarang) or from January to March (late Birak to Bunuru). The ripe, globular fruit is a pale green and yellow with a tinge of purple. In Western Australia, Oondoroo grows in an area from Perth out to Kalgoorlie and down to Esperance (eFlora.SA, 2018; FloraBase, 2018). It also grows in South Australia, Victoria and New South Wales (Atlas of Living Australia, 2018).

Culinary Uses The fruits of the Oondoroo are edible when ripe and have fallen to the ground (Cribb and Cribb, 1983;

Maiden, 1889). Although no toxicity has been reported for this plant, it is a member of the Nightshade family and eating the unripe fruit should be avoided (Maiden, 1889; Natural Medicinal Herbs, n.d.).

Pale Grass-lily

Botanical Name *Caesia micrantha* Lindl.

Noongar Name Karhrh (Apace WA, n.d.b).

Field Notes Pale Grass-lily is a tufted, perennial plant whose rootstock has both rhizomes and tubers. It grows to 0.6 m in height. It has long, thin leaves that grow from the base and pale purple flowers with six petals that appear from September to November (late Djilba through Kambarang). The Pale Grass-lily is endemic to the south-west of Western Australia and is found from Geraldton to Albany (FloraBase, 2018).

Culinary Uses The tubers of the Pale Grass-lily are edible and were roasted in hot ashes before eating (Meagher, 1975).

Family Hemerocallidaceae R.Br.

Botanical Name *Juncus pallidus* R.Br.

Noongar name Tangil (Greenskills, n.d.).

Field Notes Pale Rush is a rhizomatous, perennial, water-loving plant that grows in tufts up to 2 m in height. It has pale green stems that are approximately 8 mm in diameter. Its leaves are long, broad sheaths that grow from the base of the plant. A single cluster of straw-coloured flowers appear almost at the top of the stems from October to December (Kambarang to Birak). Pale Rush grows around swamps and watercourses all over the south-west of Western Australia from Geraldton to Esperance (FloraBase, 2018). It is also found in South Australia, Victoria, Tasmania and New South Wales (Atlas of Living Australia, 2018).

Culinary Uses The white sheaths at the base of the leaves of Pale Rush are edible.

Family Juncaceae Juss.

Other Uses The leaves were dried and used to weave mats and baskets. The stalks of the plant make a handy stick for carrying fish (Greenskills, n.d.).

Botanical Name *Calandrinia polyandra* Benth.

Noongar Name Not known.

Field Notes Parakeelya is a succulent, annual herb that spreads along the ground and grows to around 4 cm high. It has linear, fleshy leaves and deep pink flowers approximately 35 mm in diameter, with a striking yellow centre. The flowers are present from July to October (late Makuru to early Kambarang). Parakeelya is usually found in sand or loam on floodplains or stony plains (FloraBase, 2018). Parakeelya is endemic to Western Australia and is found from Exmouth to Esperance and out east into South Australia, the Northern Territory and south-west Queensland (Atlas of Living Australia, 2018).

Culinary Uses The leaves of Parakeelya are edible and can be eaten raw in a salad or steamed (Australian Plants Society, S.A. Inc. 2018).

Family Montiaceae Raf.

Passion Berry

Family Solanaceae Juss.

Botanical Name *Solanum cleistogamum* Symon, also known as *Solanum ellipticum*.

Other Common Names Wild Gooseberry and Passionberry.

Noongar Name Not known.

Field Notes Passion Berry grows as a prickly ground cover with stems up to 60 cm long. It has mid-green, soft, hairy, diamond-shaped leaves that are generally incurved. Small, insignificant purple flowers are present from September to December (late Djilba to early Birak). The fruits of the Passion Berry are globular berries 10 to 13 mm in diameter that hang in great numbers. They are creamy yellow in colour when ripe (Outback Pride, 2015). Passion Berry is found in every state of Australia except the cooler Victoria and Tasmania. In

the south-west, it is found around Geraldton and in the drier areas of Noongar country around the Avon Wheatbelt (Atlas of Living Australia, 2018; FloraBase, 2018).

Culinary Uses The fruits of Passion Berry are edible when ripe. They are reported to taste somewhere between banana, caramel and vanilla (eFlora.SA, 2017; Outback Pride, 2015).

Botanical Name *Amyema fitzgeraldii* (Blakely) Danser.

Noongar Name Nyilla Nyilla (the generic Noongar name for mistletoe).

Field Notes Pincushion Mistletoe is a hemiparasitic plant that is only found twining around the branches of and feeding off Jam Wattle trees (*Acacia acuminata*). It has pale green, elliptical to oblong leaves and green flowers with what look like red pins protruding from the centre of the flower. The flowers appear from April to October (Djeran to Kambarang). Its fruits are globular berries (karlburi) which are red when ripe. Pincushion Mistletoe can be found in abundance around Geraldton and One Arm Point but is scarcer inland around Newman and Kalgoorlie. Only the Amangu Noongars south of Geraldton would have had access to the fruit of this plant (FloraBase, 2018).

Family Loranthaceae Juss.

Culinary Uses The fruits of Pincushion Mistletoe are edible and would have been a good snack food for the Amangu Noongars (Meagher, 1975).

Pink Beaufortia

Family Myrtaceae Juss.

Botanical Name *Beaufortia schaueri* Schauer.

Noongar Name Not known.

Field Notes Pink Beaufortia is an erect or spreading shrub that grows to around 1.2 m in height. Its leaves are linear and crowded on the branches. Its pink or purple, bottlebrush-type flowers appear from June to January (Makuru to late Birak). It is found in sandy, often stony soils on plains and slopes. Pink Beaufortia is endemic to the south-west of Western Australia and is found along the coast from Albany to Israelite Bay and inland as far as the Avon Wheatbelt and Coolgardie (FloraBase, 2018).

Culinary Uses Pink Beaufortia was an excellent source of nectar (ngonyang) for Noongars who lived along the south coast and inland. They sucked the nectar directly from the flower or soaked the flowers in water to make a sweet drink.

Pink Fairy Orchid

Family Orchidaceae Juss.

Botanical Name *Caladenia latifolia* R.Br.

Noongar Names Kar and Kararr are the generic Noongar names for *Caladenia* sp. (City of Joohnalup, 2011).

Field Notes Pink Fairy Orchid is a tuberous, perennial plant growing up to 45 cm in height. It has a single leaf arising from the ground at the base of the plant up to 15 cm long. Its pink or white, star-shaped flowers with five petals appear from August to October (Djilba to early Kambarang). This plant is very coastal and is found in the south-west of Western Australia from Geraldton to beyond Esperance (FloraBase, 2018). It is also found in the southern reaches of South Australia and Victoria and in the coastal areas of Tasmania (Atlas of Living Australia, 2018).

Culinary Uses The tubers of the Pink Fairy Orchid were eaten by Noongars either raw or roasted in hot ashes.

Sometimes the tubers were pounded and formed into cakes, which were then baked in hot ashes (City of Joondalup, 2011; Maiden, 1889; Rippey and Rowland, 2004).

Botanical Name *Gastrodia lacista* D.L.Jones, formerly *Gastrodia sesamoides*.

Other Common Names Native Potato, Bell Orchid and Cinnamon Bells.

Noongar Name Koon (Whitehurst, 1997).

Field Notes The Potato Orchid is a small, tuberous, perennial plant that grows to around 50 cm in height. It is devoid of green colouring and is thought to be epiparasitic (a parasite that feeds off another parasite). Each plant can bear up to thirty flowers that are white and bell-shaped with a brown tinge on the outside of the flower. The plant flowers from November to January (late Kambarang to Birak). The Potato Orchid has a larger tuber than most other orchids, hence the name. This plant is only found around the coast in the very bottom corner of Western Australia between

Family Orchidaceae Juss.

Bunbury and Albany (FloraBase 2018; Terrestrial Orchids of South-West Australia, 2014).

Culinary Uses The swollen underground rhizomes of the Potato Orchid are edible and a good source of starch. They were eaten by Noongars either raw or roasted in hot ashes (Australian National Botanic Gardens, 2012; Cribb and Cribb, 1974; Maiden, 1889).

Family Chenopodiaceae Vent.

Botanical Name *Salsola australis* R.Br., also known as *Salsola tragus* and *Salsola kali*.

Other Common Names Buckbush, Prickly Roly-poly, Roly-poly, Russian Thistle, Saltwort, Soft Roly-poly and Tumbleweed.

Noongar Name Not known.

Field Notes Prickly Saltwort, as the name suggests, is a small, prickly, erect, biennial shrub that grows to around 1 m in height. It has small, cylindrical leaves and dry fruit with papery wings that appear from spring to autumn (Djilba to Djeran). Its small, white, translucent flowers have a pink centre. They appear from March to May (late Bunuru to Djeran) or from July to September (late Makuru to Djilba). The shrub breaks off at the base in strong winds and is blown about in the wind like tumbleweed. This plant is found all

over every state of Australia except Tasmania. It is also found in other countries (FloraBase, 2018; HerbiGuide, 2014; Rippey and Rowland, 2004).

Culinary Uses The leaves and shoots of the Prickly Saltwort can be eaten as a vegetable when boiled or steamed (Rippey and Rowland, 2004). Some cultures eat the leaves raw in salads. They also eat the seeds roasted (Natural Medicinal Herbs, 2017).

Other Uses Prickly Saltwort is reported to have medicinal uses as a diuretic and as a de-worming agent (Rippey and Rowland, 2004). Poultices of the chewed plants have been applied to ant, bee and wasp stings. Infusions (teas) of the ashes of the burned plants have been used both internally and as a wash in the treatment of smallpox and influenza (Natural Medicinal Herbs, 2017).

Botanical Name *Dichopogon capillipes* (Endl.) Brittan, formerly *Arthropodium capillipes*.

Noongar Name Adjiko (Nannup, N., in discussion with the author, July 2018).

Field Notes Purple Lily is a small, tuberous, perennial plant that grows to 1 m in height. Its long thin leaves can be up to 30 cm long. Its purple-pink flowers, sometimes up to four to a thin stem, appear from September to December (late Djilba to early Birak) or from January to March (late Birak to Bunuru). This plant is only found in the south-west of Western Australia, in coastal and near-coastal habitats, from Geraldton to Albany (FloraBase, 2018).

Culinary Uses The tubers of the Purple Lily were eaten by Noongars either raw, steamed in an earth oven or roasted in hot ashes (City of Joondalup, 2011).

Family Asparagaceae Juss.

Botanical Name *Sowerbaea laxiflora* Lindl.

Other Common Name Vanilla Lily.

Noongar Name Not known.

Field Notes Purple Tassels is a tufted perennial plant that grows to 60 cm in height. It has long, thin leaves and purple or white flowers at the end of thin, red stems. The flowers appear from August to November (Djilba to Kambarang). This plant is only found in the south-west corner of Western Australia in coastal or near-coastal habitats from Geraldton to Albany (FloraBase, 2018).

Culinary Uses The roots (bwoor) of the Purple Tassells plant were eaten by Noongars either raw, steamed in an earth oven or roasted in hot ashes (City of Joondalup, 2011).

Family Asparagaceae Juss.

Family Portulacaceae Juss.

Botanical Name *Portulaca oleracea* L.

Other Common Names Common Purslane and Pigweed.

Noongar Name Not known.

Field Notes Purslane is a ground-hugging, annual plant with red stems and small, succulent, ovate, green leaves about 25 mm long. Small, yellow flowers appear at the leaf base from April to May (Djeran) (FloraBase, 2018). This plant is found all over Australia except for Tasmania (Atlas of Living Australia, 2018).

Culinary Uses The tiny black seeds of Purslane were ground to make flour for damper (mereny). The leaves and stems can be eaten raw, boiled or steamed as a green vegetable. The raw leaves are reported to taste like lettuce (Coppin, 2008; Cribb and Cribb, 1974; Isaacs, 1992; Maiden,

1889). Some groups carried Purslane leaves with them on walks from one camp to another as a source of moisture when water was scarce (Dann, 2003).

Quandong

Family Santalaceae R.Br.

Botanical Name *Santalum acuminatum* (R.Br.) A.DC.

Other Common Names Sandalwood, Desert Quandong, Sweet Quandong and Native Peach.

Noongar Names Dumbari (SERCUL, 2014), Wongup (Wheatbelt NRM, 2015) Jawirli, Walku, Wanga, Wayanu, Wongil (Coppin, 2008), Candang, Wong, Wonyill, Wolgol (Bindon and Chadwick, 2011; Abbott, 1983) and Worinj (Goode et al, 2015).

Field Notes The Quandong is one of many types of sandalwood. It is semi-parasitic and grows as a large shrub or small tree to 7 m in height. It has long, thin greyish-green leaves and a rough bark. The small white flowers of the Quandong occur in clusters from January to April (late Birak through Bunuru to early Djeran) or July to September (Makuru and Djilba) or November to December (late

Kambarang to early Birak). After it flowers fleshy fruits appear that are bright red when ripe. The round seeds (gunnar) inside the fruits have a hard, woody shell (Australian Native Plants Society (Australia), 2018). Quandong grows in many parts of Australia from coastal south-west Western Australia, across the southern reaches of the Northern Territory, most of South Australia, to New South Wales and south-western Queensland (Australian National Botanic Gardens, 2015). In Western Australia, it is found all over the south-west from Shark bay to Esperance and east out past Kalgoorlie (FloraBase, 2018).

Culinary Uses The fruits of Quandong made a tasty snack for Noongars. The fruits were often dried and stored for later use. The early settlers made pies and jams from the fruits. Inside the fruit is a nut which has a kernel inside that can be roasted and eaten (Cribb and Cribb, 1974; Daw et al, 2011; Low, 1991; Maiden, 1889; SERCUL, 2014).

Other Uses The seed kernels were ground and mixed with animal fat and used as a liniment for sore muscles. The leaves were pounded to a paste and applied to sores and boils. The pounded leaves were also used to treat gonorrhoea before the advent of antibiotics (Lassak and McCarthy, 2008). Infusions of the leaves, made by soaking the leaves in water, were taken internally to treat diabetes. A paste made from the ground seeds can be used as a skin moisturiser.

Family Orchidaceae Juss.

Botanical Name *Pyrorchis nigricans* (R.Br.) D.L.Jones and M.A. Clem.

Other Common Names Undertaker Orchid, Potato Orchid and Elephant's Ears.

Noongar Names Djubak (Coppin, 2008; Daw et al, 2011) and Djubag (Goode et al, 2015).

Field Notes Red Beaks are tuberous, perennial plants that grow to 30 cm in height. They have large, ear-shaped leaves that arise from the base of the plant and red, beak-shaped flowers that appear from August to October (Djilba to early Kambarang). In Western Australia, Red Beaks are found in coastal and near-coastal habitats from Shark Bay to Esperance (FloraBase, 2018). They are also found in South Australia, Victoria, Tasmania and southern New South Wales (Atlas of Living Australia, 2018).

Culinary Uses The tuberous roots (bwoor) of Red Beaks are high in starch and were eaten by Noongars either raw or roasted in hot ashes, or pounded and made into cakes that were baked in hot ashes. The roots are reported to taste like potato (City of Joondalup, 2011; Coppin, 2008; Daw et al, 2011; Explore Melville, 2012).

Ribbon Pea

Botanical Name *Leptosema aphyllum* (Hook.) Crisp, formerly *Brachysema aphyllum*.

Noongar Name Not known.

Field Notes Ribbon Pea is a prostrate or erect, spreading shrub that grows to 1 m in height. It has long, green, lanceolate leaves on long stems and red horn-shaped flowers that are light-yellow near the stem. The flowers are present from May to October (late Djeran to early Kambarang). This plant is only found in Western Australia on the Geraldton Sandplains and in the Avon Wheatbelt (FloraBase, 2018).

Culinary Uses The flowers of Ribbon Pea were another good source of nectar (ngonyang) for Noongars, who usually sucked the nectar straight from the flower (Meagher, 1975).

Family Fabaceae Lindl.

Round-leaf Pigface

Botanical Name *Disphyma crassifolium* subsp. *clavellatum* (Haw.) Chinnock.

Other Common Name Rounded Noon-flower.

Noongar Name Not known.

Field Notes Round-leaf Pigface is a ground-hugging, succulent plant similar in appearance to Coastal Pigface (*Carpobrotus virescens*), the difference being Round-leaf Pigface has rounded leaves whereas Coastal Pigface has angled ones. Its attractive round flowers are about 5 cm across and pink, violet or mauve in colour. The flowers appear from January to February (Birak to early Bunuru), in May (late Djeran) or from August to December (Djilba to early Birak). The fruit of the Round-leaf Pigface is a reddish-brown capsule with flaps that open at the top when ripe. Round-leaf Pigface grows in a variety of soils including sand, sandy loam, clay

Family Aizoaceae Martinov

and clay loam, both in coastal areas around Geraldton, Albany and Esperance but also inland out beyond Kalgoorlie (Archer, 2018; FloraBase, 2018). It is also found in South Australia, Victoria, southern New South Wales and Tasmania (Atlas of Living Australia, 2018).

Culinary Uses The leaves of the Round-leaf Pigface are edible and can be eaten raw or cooked. They are reported to have a slight salty taste (Kapitany, 2015). The fruits are also edible (City of Charles Sturt, n.d.).

Botanical Name *Solanum orbiculatum* Poir. subsp. *Orbiculatum.*

Other Common Name Wild Tomato.

Noongar Name Not known.

Field Notes Round-leaved Solanum is a shrub that grows to around 1.5 m in height. It has grey-green, ovate leaves to 60 mm in length. Its purple-violet flowers have five petals and prominent bright yellow stamens. They appear from June to October (Makuru to early Kambarang). The fruits are globular, up to 15 mm in diameter and are a pale-yellow colour when ripe. This plant is endemic to Western Australia, growing near the coast around Geraldton and Shark Bay and inland into the Northern Territory and South Australia (Atlas of Living Australia, 2018; eFlora.SA, 2018; FloraBase, 2018).

Family Solanaceae Juss.

Culinary Uses The fruits of the Round-leaved Solanum are edible when ripe (Johnson and Ahmed, 2005).

Family Chenopodiaceae Vent.

Botanical Name *Tecticornia verrucosa* Paul G.Wilson.

Noongar Name Milyu is the generic Noongar name for Samphire (Moore, 1884a; Parks and Wildlife Service, 2018).

Field Notes Samphire is a leafless, perennial or annual, succulent plant that grows to around 6 cm in height. Its small, purple flowers appear from August to September (Djilba). This plant is found in most areas of Western Australia except for the south-west coast (FloraBase, 2018). It is also found in the southern reaches of the Northern Territory (Atlas of Living Australia, 2018).

Culinary Uses The small black seeds were harvested by Indigenous Australians and ground into flour, which was mixed with water to make damper (mereny) (Kapitany, 2015; Useful Tropical Plants, 2015).

Sandalwood

Botanical Name *Santalum spicatum* (R.Br.) A.DC.

Noongar Names Willarak (Moore, 1884b), Uilarac, Waang, Wolgol and Wollgat (Abbott, 1983).

Field Notes Sandalwood grows as a small tree up to 5 m in height. It is a parasitic plant that feeds off the roots of trees nearby, usually Acacias such as Jam Wattle (*Acacia acuminata*). The grey-green leaves are ovate to lanceolate and are tapered at both ends. The flowers, which have four red petals and a green centre, are present from February to June (Bunuru to Makuru). Its orange fruits are spherical and about 3 cm in diameter. The fruit has a kernel with a hard shell. The fruit is present from August to December (Djilba to early Birak) (Florabank, 2018; FloraBase, 2018). Sandalwood is found in the drier parts of the south-west of Western Australia from Shark Bay down and east out past Newman,

Wiluna, Kalgoorlie and Norseman. It is also found in South Australia from the border with Western Australia to the Flinders Ranges (Atlas of Living Australia, 2018; Florabank, 2018). It used to grow around the Perth region but has been harvested to extinction in this area (Cunningham, 1998).

Culinary Uses The kernels of the fruits of Sandalwood are edible and were eaten by Noongars raw or roasted in hot ashes (Florabank, 2018). The bark of the roots can also be eaten (Maiden, 1889).

Other Uses Decoctions (teas) made from the inner bark (boort) of Sandalwood were drunk as a cough mixture or for bronchitis. The oil from the nuts was used as a rubbing medicine for colds and stiffness and for skin rashes (Lassak and McCarthy, 2008). The crushed leaves were applied as a poultice to burns, scalds and sores (Cunningham, 1998).

Botanical Name *Beaufortia squarrosa* Schauer.

Other Common Name Sand Bottlebrush.

Noongar Name Buno (Abbott, 1983).

Field Notes Sand Beaufortia is an erect, evergreen shrub that grows to around 2 m in height. Its small, ovate leaves are approximately 8 mm long. Its fruit are woody capsules 4 to 6 mm long. It produces red, orange or yellow bottlebrush-type flowers from late August to May (Djilba to Djeran). Sand Beaufortia is found in sandy soils on sandplains that are often associated with winter-wet depressions. It is native to the south-west of Western Australia and is only found from Geraldton to Albany (FloraBase, 2018).

Culinary Uses Sand Beaufortia was another excellent source of nectar (ngonyang) for Noongars, who either sucked

Family Myrtaceae Juss.

the nectar directly from the flower or soaked the flowers
in water to make a sweet drink called mungitch (City of
Joondalup, 2011).

Family Aizoaceae Martinov.

Botanical Name *Sarcozona praecox* (F.Muell.) S.T.Blake.

Other Common Name Pigface.

Noongar Names Kolbogo, Mejarak, Manbibi (Macintyre, K., in discussion with the author, March 2019) and Pain (Bindon and Chadwick, 2011).

Field Notes Sarcozona looks like Coastal Pigface (*Carpobrotus virescens*) but the leaves are slightly different in cross section and this plant prefers the drier areas inland whereas Coastal Pigface is very coastal. Sarcozona is a sprawling succulent shrub that grows to around 0.3 m in height. Its succulent leaves are triangular in cross-section and can be up to 10 cm in length. Its pink, white or purple flowers have many petals and appear from July to September (late Makuru and Djilba). Its succulent fruits are reddish in colour when ripe. Sarcozona is found in the drier areas of Western

Australia from Geraldton to Esperance (FloraBase, 2018). It is also found in South Australia, Victoria and New South Wales (Atlas of Living Australia, 2018; Lucid Key Server, 2015).

Culinary Uses The fleshy fruits of the Sarcozona plant are edible (Cribb and Cribb, 1974).

Scarlet Runner

Botanical Name *Kennedia prostrata* R.Br.

Other Common Name Running Postman.

Noongar Names Wollung, Pulbarn (Moore, 1884b), Kuralo (Bindon and Chadwick, 1992) and Wollong (Perth Region NRM, n.d.b).

Field Notes Scarlet Runner grows as a prostrate ground cover with a spread of approximately 2.5 m. Its grey-green leaves have three segments and wavy yellow edges. Its pea-shaped, bright red flowers appear from April to November (Djeran to late Kambarang). Flat seed pods about 50 mm long are present when flowering finishes. Scarlet Runner grows throughout the south-west from Geraldton to Esperance. It is also found in South Australia, Victoria, Tasmania and New South Wales (Atlas of Living Australia, 2018; Australian Native Plants Society, 2018).

Family Fabaceae Lindl.

Culinary Uses The flowers of Scarlet Runner were another good source of nectar (ngonyang) for Noongars, who sucked the nectar straight from the flowers. A tea can be made from the leaves, which are reported to have a mild liquorice flavour (Cribb and Cribb, 1974; Gott, 2010; SERCUL, 2014).

Other Uses The nectar from the flowers was used to soothe sore throats (Hansen and Horsfall, 2016).

Botanical Name *Exocarpos odoratus* (Miq.) A.DC.

Noongar Names Dtulya (Moore, 1884a) and Jackitup (Bindon and Chadwick, 1992).

Field Notes Scented Ballart grows as a small shrub to 1.5 m in height. It is hemiparasitic on the roots of nearby trees. It has ovate, succulent leaves and small, yellow-green flowers that can appear anytime throughout the year. Scented Ballart prefers grey sand or sandy clay on coastal dunes or coastal cliffs. It is indigenous to the coastal strip of the south-west of Western Australia from Busselton to Albany (FloraBase, 2018).

Culinary Uses The fruits of Scented Ballart are edible but are reported to be tasteless (Moore, 1884b).

Family Santalaceae R.Br.

Botanical name *Urtica incisa* Poir.

Other Common Name Stinging Nettle.

Noongar Name Not known.

Field Notes Scrub Nettle is an upright perennial plant that grows to around 1 m in height. Its leaf shape can vary from ovate to lanceolate and range from 5 to 10 cm in length. The leaves have serrated edges and deep veins. Its stems are covered with stinging hairs that inject formic acid and other stinging chemicals. Its small, green flowers are found on slender spikes from July to January (late Makuru to late Birak) (Rankmore, 2013). Scrub Nettle prefers rainforest areas that have been disturbed and wetter forest creek beds (Rankmore, 2013). Scrub Nettle grows more prolifically in the eastern states from southern Queensland through Victoria, Tasmania and South Australia. In Western Australia

Family Urticaceae Juss.

it is indigenous to the Esperance Sandplains (Atlas of Living Australia, 2018; FloraBase, 2018).

Culinary Uses The leaves of Scrub Nettle are edible and were eaten by some Aboriginal groups, who would bake them over hot stones before eating them (Low, 1991).

Other Uses The stinging hairs were placed onto areas, especially the joints, that were affected by arthritis and rheumatism. The stinging of the chemicals would stimulate blood flow around the area that was affected, and pain would be eased (Rankmore, 2013). Early settlers drank decoctions (teas) of the leaves as a tonic (Low, 1991).

Family Chenopodiaceae Vent.

Botanical Name *Rhagodia baccata* subsp. *dioica* (Nees) Paul G.Wilson.

Other Common Name Berry Saltbush.

Noongar Name Not known.

Field Notes Sea Berry Saltbush grows as a spreading shrub to 4 m in height. It has small, light green elliptical leaves. Its small, cream-yellow flowers appear in a panicle or cluster from February to May (Bunuru to Djeran) or from October to December (Kambarang to Birak). After flowering small red berries (karlburi) appear. Sea Berry Saltbush is a very coastal plant that thrives in sand dunes, coastal rocky areas and adjacent hills. It is found around the coast from Geraldton to Albany (FloraBase, 2018).

Culinary Uses The small red berries (karlburi) of
Sea Berry Saltbush are edible and made a nice snack for the
Noongars. The leaves can be boiled or steamed and eaten as
a vegetable. The leaves are said to taste a bit like slightly salty
spinach (Daw et al, 2011; Explore Melville, 2012).

Family Chenopodiaceae Vent.

Botanical Name *Suaeda australis* (R.Br.) Moq.

Other Common Name Austral Seablite.

Noongar Name Not known.

Field Notes Seablight is a perennial plant that grows to around 90 cm in height. It has a spreading habit and branching occurs from the base. The succulent, light green to purplish-red flattened leaves can be up to 40 mm long. Its small, green flowers appear from January to October (late Birak to early Kambarang) (FloraBase, 2018). In Western Australia Seablight is found around the coast from Geraldton to Esperance. It is also found in coastal areas in all other Australian states except the Northern Territory (Atlas of Living Australia, 2018).

Culinary Uses The leaves of Seablight can be eaten as a green vegetable either boiled or steamed. Early settlers used to pickle the leaves to preserve them (Cribb and Cribb, 1974; Kapitany, 2015; Low, 1991).

Botanical Name *Apium prostratum* Vent.

Noongar Name Not known.

Field Notes Sea Celery is a prostrate or erect biennial or perennial plant that grows to 1 m in height. Its green leaves are segmented. Its small white or pink flowers appear in clusters at the end of stalks anytime from August to April (Djilba to early Djeran). Sea Celery prefers coastal and near-coastal habitats. In Western Australia, it grows around Geraldton then from Perth to Esperance (Australian Native Plants Society (Australia), 2018; FloraBase, 2018). It also grows in South Australia, Victoria, Tasmania, New South Wales and Southern Queensland (Atlas of Living Australia, 2018).

Family Apiaceae Lindl.

Culinary Uses The stems and leaves of Sea Celery are edible. It is usually eaten cooked and is reported to taste like common celery (*Apium graveolens*) (Australian Native Plants Society (Australia), 2017; Cribb and Cribb, 1974; Gott, 2010; Low, 1991).

Sheoak

Botanical Name *Allocasuarina fraseriana* (Miq.)
L.A.S.Johnson.

Other Common Names Western Sheoak
and Common Sheoak.

Noongar Names Kondil (Perth Region NRM, 2015), Condil
(Abbott, 1983), Kulli, Gulli (Greenskills, n.d.), Quail and Kwell
(Bindon and Chadwick, 1992).

Field Notes Sheoak is a tree that grows to a height of
about 15 m. Exposure to salty coastal breezes can stunt its
growth. Its slender green branchlets, informally referred to as
'needles', are more correctly termed cladodes. The cladodes
are segmented, and the true leaves are tiny teeth encircling
each joint. Male trees of this species have small brown flower
spikes at the end of branchlets. Flowering is prolific, giving
male trees a rusty brown hue during flowering in late winter

and early spring (Djilba to early Kambarang). The female trees of the species bear small flowers on short branchlets of their own. Fertilised flowers develop egg-shaped cones from 1.5 to 3.5 cm in diameter. Sheoaks prefer lateritic soil or sand in Jarrah forests or near the coast in woodland and open forests. Sheoak is indigenous to the south-west of Western Australia and occurs in coastal areas from Jurien Bay to Albany (Flora of Australia online, 2018).

Culinary Uses The young cones of the Sheoak were eaten by Noongars as a snack food (Hansen and Horsfall, 2016).

Other Uses Noongar women (yorgas) often gave birth under Sheoak trees because of the softness of the needles (cladodes). The Sheoak needles were also used for bedding in shelters (mia mias) covered with kangaroo-skin cloaks (buka). This combination made a very comfortable bed (Hansen and Horsfall, 2016).

Family Myrtaceae Juss.

Botanical Name *Calothamnus sanguineus* Labill.

Noongar Name Pin-dak (City of Bayswater, 2010).

Field Notes Silky-leaved Blood Flower grows as an erect or open spreading shrub to a height of up to 2 m. It has needle-like leaves with sharp tips. Its flowers have small green-yellow petals that are unremarkable but beautiful, and red stamens that hang down like a claw. The flowers appear from March to November (late Bunuru to Kambarang). This plant is only found in the south-west of Western Australia in both coastal and inland habitats from Geraldton to Albany (FloraBase, 2018).

Culinary Uses The flowers of the Silky-leaved Blood Flower were another good source of nectar (ngonyang) for Noongars, who either sucked the nectar directly from the flower or soaked the flowers in water to make a sweet

drink. The resulting liquid was often left to ferment into an intoxicating liquor they called gep (City of Joondalup, 2011).

Silver Cassia

Botanical Name *Senna artemisioides* (DC.) Randell.

Other Common Names Feathery Cassia, Punty Bush, Limestone Senna, Desert Cassia and Silver Senna.

Noongar Name Not known.

Field Notes Silver Cassia is a shrub with many sub-species that grows to around 3 m in height. It has ovate leaves around 4 cm long that are covered with tiny hairs, giving the leaves a silvery appearance. Its small yellow flowers are approximately 1 cm across. They are usually present from April to November (Djeran to late Kambarang). Its fruit are pods about 8 cm long. Silver Cassia grows in most soil types in a variety of habitats in all Australian states and territories including Tasmania. In the south-west it is found mainly in the drier areas (FloraBase, 2018; Oz Native Plants, 2018).

Family Fabaceae Lindl.

Culinary Uses The seeds of the Silver Cassia are edible and Noongars probably ground them into flour to make damper (mereny) (Wild Magazine, 2018).

Small Leaf Clematis

Family Ranunculaceae Juss.

Botanical Name *Clematis linearifolia* Steud., formerly *Clematis microphylla*.

Other Common Names Small Clematis, Old Man's Beard (Lassak and McCarthy, 2008), Slender Clematis and Traveller's Joy.

Noongar Name Taaruk (Coppin, 2008; Daw et al, 2011).

Field Notes Small Leaf Clematis is a climbing plant with wiry stems that grows to approximately 5 m in length. The plant is usually found draped over a small host shrub. Its leaves are distinctly three-lobed, with each lobe linear to narrow, lance-shaped, and up to 6 cm long and 2 cm wide. Its creamy-white, star-shaped flowers with four petals and spiky long stamens appear from July to October (Makuru to Kambarang) (Archer, 2018; Flora of Australia Online, 2018). Archer (2018) relates that Small Leaf Clematis is 'especially

plentiful in and around hollows, lakes and flats between stable tertiary dunes, where it can look quite spectacular draped over other shrubs and spreading to around 5 m'. Small Leaf Clematis is only found in the south-west of Western Australia on coastal sandplains from Shark Bay to Augusta and around the Esperance area (FloraBase, 2018).

Culinary Uses The roots (bwoor) of Small Leaf Clematis are edible. They were usually roasted in hot ashes before pounding them into a paste that was then formed into cakes which were baked again in hot ashes. The roots are reported to be high in protein as well as starch (Coppin, 2008; Daw et al, 2011; De Angeles, 2005; Gott, 2010).

Family Proteaceae Juss.

Botanical Names *Persoonia longifolia* R.Br., *Persoonia saccata* R.Br. and *Persoonia elliptica* R.Br.

Other Common Names Snottygobble (*Persoonia longifolia*), Pouched Snottygobble (*Persoonia saccata*) and Spreading Snottygobble (*Persoonia elliptica*).

Noongar Names Kadgeegurr, Ngowdik (Moore, 1884a) and Cadgeegurrup.

Field Notes There are a few varieties of Snottygobble that grow in the south-west of Western Australia: Snottygobble (*Persoonia longifolia*), Pouched Snottygobble (*Persoonia saccata*) and Spreading Snottygobble (*Persoonia elliptica*) are three that are known to have edible fruit and there are probably more. They grow as an erect shrub or tree to between 5 to 8 m in height. Their dark green leaves vary from long and narrow to eliptical. *Persoonia longifolia*

has rough, flaky bark that is a dark red colour with deep vertical grooves on the trunk. *Persoonia saccata* has smooth bark that is sometimes flaky towards the base. The bark of *Persoonia elliptica* has been described as grey and corky. The yellow-orange flowers of *Persoonia longifolia* appear from November through to February (Kambarang to early Bunuru). The green-yellow flowers of *Persoonia saccata* and *Persoonia elliptica* appear from July to February (late Makuru to early Buburu). The spherical to elliptical fruits appear in summer and autumn (Birak to Djeran) and are green initially but turn yellow as they ripen (Perth Seed, 2010). All three Snottygobbles mentioned are endemic to the south-west of Western Australia and grow in coastal and near-coastal habitats from Perth to Albany (FloraBase, 2018).

Culinary Uses The fruits of these Snottygobbles are edible and were enjoyed by coastal Noongars. The fruits contain sweet pulp that resembles snot, hence the name (Coppin, 2008; Cribb and Cribb, 1974; Low, 1991; Maiden, 1889; Roleybushcare, 2015).

Other Uses Decoctions (teas) of the bark (boort) of *Persoonia longifolia,* made by boiling the crushed bark in water, were applied externally to the skin to relieve skin disorders. They were also used as an eyewash. Infusions of the leaves made by crushing the leaves and soaking them in water were taken internally to relieve colds and sore throats (Hansen and Horsfall, 2016).

Botanical Name *Kunzea ericifolia* (Sm.) Heynh.

Other Common Names Yellow Kunzea and Native Tea.

Noongar Names Kitja Boorn, Poorndil Condi (City of Joondalup, 2011) and Pondil (Perth Region NRM, 2015).

Field Notes Spearwood is an erect shrub that grows up to 4 m in height. Its leaves are a linear form growing to a length of about 10 mm and a width of 1 mm. The leaves cover almost all of the stems. Small, round, yellow or cream-white flowers are present from July to December (late Makuru to early Birak). Spearwood is endemic to the south-west of Western Australia and is found in sandy soils in seasonally wet swamps and other moist situations and amongst rocks on summits from Perth to Esperance (FloraBase, 2018).

Family Myrtaceae Juss.

Culinary Uses Spearwood flowers would have been another good source of nectar (ngonyang) for Noongars. Early settlers made tea from the leaves, which they found to be not only pleasant to drink but also a good tonic (City of Joondalup, 2011).

Other Uses As the common name suggests, Noongars used the limbs of the Spearwood to make spears for hunting game (City of Joondalup, 2011).

Spider Flower

Botanical Name *Grevillea vestita* (Endl.) Meisn.

Other Common Names Grey Grevillea and Toothbrush.

Noongar Name Not known.

Field Notes Spider Flower either grows as an erect or spreading prickly shrub, to around 3 m in height and, if spreading, up to 3.5 m wide. It has green lanceolate leaves about 50 mm long and white to pale pink, spikey flowers that appear in clusters at the end of its branches from June to November (Makuru to Kambarang) (Australian Native Plants Society (Australia), 2018). *Grevillea vestita* is endemic to the south-west of Western Australia and is found all along the coast from Geraldton to Dunsborough (FloraBase, 2018).

Family Proteaceae Juss.

Culinary Uses Spider Flower was another source of nectar (ngonyang) for Noongars, who either sucked the nectar directly from the flower or made a sweet drink by soaking the flowers in water (City of Joondalup, 2011).

Family Proteaceae Juss.

Botanical Name *Grevillea preissii* Meisn.

Noongar name Not known.

Field Notes Spider Net Grevillea grows as a small, erect or prostrate shrub to 1.7 m in height. Its needle-like leaves are greyish-green, around 6 cm long and divide into two or more lobes near the centre. It develops beautiful red spider-like flowers from June to September (Makuru to Djilba) (Australian Native Plants Society (Australia), 2018). This shrub is endemic to the south-west of Western Australia and is found along the coast from Geraldton to Bunbury (FloraBase, 2018).

Culinary Uses The flowers of the Spider Net Grevillea were another good source of nectar (ngonyang) for Noongars, who either sucked the nectar directly from the flower or soaked the flowers in water to make a sweet drink. The

resulting liquid was often left to ferment into an intoxicating liquor Noongars called gep (City of Joondalup, 2011).

Botanical Name *Caladenia* spp.

Noongar Names Kara (Perth Region NRM, n.d.b), Kahta-ninda-yootah (Chadwick, 1993), Kararr (Collard, 2009) and Cara (Perth Region NRM, 2015).

Field Notes The south-west corner of Western Australia is home to around 140 Spider Orchids. Examples include *Caladenia arenicola* (Carousel Spider Orchid), *Caladenia flava* (Cowslip Orchid), *Caladenia crebra* (Arrowsmith Spider Orchid), *Caladenia longicauda* (Common White Spider Orchid) and *Caladenia discoidea* (Dancing Orchid) (Orchids of South-west Australia, 2018). They all have tuberous roots and spider-like flowers that appear in the spring wildflower season (Djilba and Kambarang) (FloraBase, 2018).

Family Orchidaceae Juss.

Culinary Uses Spider Orchids were an important food source for Noongars, who ate the tuberous roots (bwoor) either raw or roasted in hot ashes. The flavour of the roots varies depending on the species (Coppin, 2008; Explore Melville, 2012; Maiden, 1889).

Botanical Name *Lepidium aschersonii* Thell.

Noongar Name Not known.

Field Notes Spiny Peppercress is a small, erect perennial herb that only grows to 30 cm in height. Its basal leaves are lobed and are up to 12 cm long. Its leaves reduce in size further up the stem. Its small white flowers are present from spring to autumn (Djilba to Bunuru). Spiny Peppercress is now exceptionally rare due to the introduction of sheep and cattle but can still be found in isolated patches on clay ridges in the south-west from Denmark to Albany (FloraBase, 2018; VicFlora, 2018). There are also isolated patches in Victoria and New South Wales (Atlas of Living Australia, 2018).

Culinary Uses All plants of the *Lepidium* species have edible leaves and stems and were eaten steamed (Coppin, 2008; Low, 1991).

Family Brassicaceae Burnett.

Botanical Name *Atriplex suberecta* I.Verd.

Other Common Name Lagoon Saltbush.

Noongar Name Not known.

Field Notes Sprawling Saltbush is a monoecious, sprawling perennial herb that branches from the base and grows to a height of 1 m. Its leaves are usually thin and narrow, up to 30 mm long, but can be wider with serrated edges in some areas. Its small, pale green flowers are approximately 2 mm wide. Male and female flowers are found on the same plant. After flowering it produces slightly flattened, red berries. Sprawling Saltbush is found growing in clay loam or sandy loam all over the south-west corner of Western Australia (Department of Primary Industries, Parks, Water and Environment, n.d.; FloraBase, 2018). It is also found in South Australia, New South Wales, Victoria and Tasmania (Atlas of Living Australia, 2018).

Culinary Uses The red berries of the Sprawling Saltbush are edible when ripe (Wildflower Society of WA, n.d.).

Family Chenopodiaceae Vent.

Stalked Mistletoe

Botanical Name *Amyema miquelii* (Miq.) Tiegh.

Other Common Names Box Mistletoe, Bronze Mistletoe, Drooping Mistletoe, Weeping Mistletoe and Mistletoe.

Noongar Name Nyilla Nyilla (the generic Noongar name for mistletoe).

Field Notes Stalked Mistletoe is a hemiparasitic, climbing plant that is usually found draped over Eucalypts or Acacias. It has long, elliptical leaves approximately 35 cm in length, and long, red, tubular flowers with up to five petals that usually appear in summer or autumn (Birak to Djeran). After flowering yellow, fleshy, elliptical fruits about 12 mm in diameter appear. The fruits are yellow to red in colour when ripe. Stalked Mistletoe is found widely distributed in all Australian states except Tasmania (Atlas of Living Australia, 2018; Australia Native Plants Society (Australia), 2018).

Family Loranthaceae Juss.

Culinary Uses The fruits of Stalked Mistletoe are edible when ripe and were a good snack food for Indigenous Australians all over mainland Australia (Cicada Woman Tours, 2013).

Botanical Name *Dodonaea viscosa* Jacq., also known as *Dodonaea angustifolia* and *Dodonaea attenuata*.

Other Common Names Desert Hopbush, Broad Leaf Hopbush, Candlewood, Narrow Leaf Hopbush, Native Hopbush, Soapwood, Switch Sorrel, Wedge Leaf Hopbush, Native Hop, Giant Hopbush and Hopbush.

Noongar Name Waning (Abbott, 1983).

Other Aboriginal Names Watchupga, Kirni and Tecan (Lassak and McCarthy, 2008).

Field Notes Sticky Hopbush is an evergreen shrub or small tree that grows to about 5 m in height. The sticky leaves vary in shape from elliptical to oblong and are reddish or purplish in colour (Lassak and McCarthy, 2001). In Western Australia, its greenish-yellow flowers appear from June to

Family Sapindaceae Juss.

August (Makuru to early Djilba). Sticky Hopbush prefers sand, loam and clay. It grows in arid and semi-arid areas in a variety of habitats. Sticky Hopbush is found throughout mainland Australia as well as Africa and many other countries throughout Europe, the Pacific islands and the Americas (Cribb and Cribb, 1983).

Culinary Uses The nectar (ngonyang) from Sticky Hopbush, when mixed with the nectar from *Kunzea* species, was mixed with water and left to ferment into an exceptionally pleasant alcoholic beverage called gep (Nannup, N., in discussion with the author, July 2018).

Other Uses The leaves were chewed to soothe toothache, though the juice was not swallowed (Lassak and McCarthy, 2001). The crushed leaves and the juice were used externally in the treatment of stonefish and stingray wounds. The juice of the crushed leaves is also reported to have antifungal and anti-inflammatory properties (Venkatesh et al., 2008). Infusions (teas) of the leaves were rubbed all over the body to reduce fevers. The leafy branches produce clean smoke, which was used to smoke babies (waving smoke over babies for therapeutic reasons), in smoking ceremonies to keep out bad spirits, and as an insect repellent (Hansen and Horsfall, 2016).

Botanical Name *Thelymitra* sp.

Noongar Name Joobuk (Goode et al, 2010).

Field Notes This genus of orchid gets its name from the habit of its flowers only opening on warm to hot days. There are around fifty species of Sun Orchids in Australia, many of which are found in the moister areas of Western Australia. Examples include *Thelymitra crinite* (Blue Lady Orchid), *Thelymitra benthamiana* (Cinnamon Sun Orchid), *Thelymitra variegata* (Queen of Sheba), *Thelymitra villosa* (Custard Orchid), *Thelymitra stellata* (Star Sun Orchid), *Thelymitra graminea* (Shy Sun Orchid – Noongar name Taaliny) and *Thelymitra tigrina* (Tiger Orchid). All these orchids are endemic to the south-west corner of Western Australia. Their flowers are usually present in the spring wildflower season (Djilba and Kambarang) and come in many colours, including

Family Orchidaceae Juss.

white, yellow, pink, red, orange, blue and purple
(Watkinson, n.d.).

Culinary Uses All the Sun Orchids of the south-west of
Western Australia have tuberous roots (bwoor) that are
edible. Noongars ate them either raw or roasted in hot ashes.
They are high in starch and are reported to taste like potato
(Explore Melville, 2012).

Swamp Bottlebrush

Family Myrtaceae Juss.

Botanical Name *Beaufortia sparsa* R.Br.

Noongar Name Not known.

Field Notes Swamp Bottlebrush is an erect or spreading shrub that grows to 3 m in height. Its flat or dished, ovate leaves are crowded on the lower stems. Bright red-orange, bottlebrush-shaped flowers appear from September to November (Djilba to Kambarang) or January to April (late Birak to early Djeran). Swamp Bottlebrush is found in sand in swampy areas and along river banks. It is only found in the south-west of Western Australia from Busselton to Albany (Atlas of Living Australia, 2018; Florabase, 2018).

Culinary Uses Swamp Bottlebrush was an excellent source of nectar (ngonyang) for Noongars who lived along the south coast. They either sucked the nectar directly from the flower or they soaked the flowers in water to make a sweet drink.

Swamp Saltbush

Botanical Name *Atriplex amnicola* Paul G.Wilson

Other Common Names Silver Saltbush and River Saltbush.

Noongar Name Not known.

Field Notes Swamp Saltbush grows as a spreading, branching shrub up to 2.5 m high and up to 4 m across. The branches may spread across the ground and take root. It has small, blue-green, ovate leaves and purplish male and female flowers that grow on separate plants. The flowers appear in July (late Makuru). Its fruits are woody pods around 5 mm square with a single seed. This plant is only found in Western Australia south and east of Karratha, out past Newman and Kalgoorlie (FloraBase, 2018).

Family Chenopodiaceae Vent.

Culinary Uses The leaves and seeds of Swamp Saltbush are edible (Gott, 2010).

Family Cyperaceae Juss.

Botanical Name *Eleocharis sphacelata* R.Br.

Other Common Names Tall Spike-rush, Kuta and Bamboo Spike Sedge.

Noongar Name Goorgogo.

Field Notes Tall Spikerush is a stout, rhizomatous, perennial, grass-like sedge that grows to 2 m in height. Its small, white flowers appear in February (Buburu) or October (Kambarang). It prefers black muddy soil in and around swamps and lakes (FloraBase, 2018). Tall Spikerush is found in all Australian states. It endemic to Western Australia and is found around swamps and watercourses from Kalumburu to Esperance. It is much more prolific in the far north of the Northern Territory and all over New South Wales, Victoria and Tasmania. (Atlas of Living Australia, 2018).

Culinary Uses The underground rhizomes of the Tall Spike-rush are high in starch and were eaten by most Indigenous Australian groups either raw or roasted in hot ashes (Coppin, 2008).

Family Scrophulariaceae Juss.

Botanical Name *Eremophila glabra* (R.Br.) Ostenf.

Other Common Name Kalbarri Carpet.

Noongar Name Berrung (a generic Noongar name for a low, flowering shrub) (City of Joondalup, 2011).

Field Notes Tar Bush can grow as either a prostrate shrub with a spread of up to 2 m, or a small erect shrub up to 1 m in height. Its ovate, or sometimes lanceolate, leaves can be grey and without hairs or grey and hairy. Its tubular flowers vary in colour and can be green, yellow, orange or red. Flowering occurs from late winter to summer (Djilba to Birak). Its fruit are ovoid to almost spherical, from 4 to 9 mm in diameter, smooth, dry or fleshy and dark brown. Tar Bush can be found in winter-wet depressions, sandplains and sand dunes all over the southern half of Western Australia (FloraBase, 2018). It is also found in the dry areas of all the other mainland

states and territories except Tasmania (Australian Native Plants Society (Australia), 2018).

Culinary Uses The seeds of Tar Bush are edible (Australian Native Nursery, n.d.).

Tassel Flower

Botanical Name *Leucopogon verticillatus* R.Br.

Other Common Names Tassel Bush and Coast Beard Heath.

Noongar Name Not known.

Field Notes Tassel Flower is an erect, bamboo-like shrub that grows to 4 m in height. The leaves form whorls around the stalk separated by gaps of 3 to 6 cm. The leaves are a light green to yellow-orange in colour and have clear veins. The flowers form tassels of pink or red on the plant from August to November (Djilba to Kambarang). Its fruit are tiny green berries (karlburi). Tassel Flower is endemic to the south-west of Western Australia where it is found in Karri, Jarrah, Tingle and similar forests from Perth to Albany (FloraBase, 2018; iNaturalist.org, n.d.).

Family Ericaceae Juss.

Culinary Uses The tiny, sweet, green berries (karlburi) of the Tassel Flower shrub were a good snack food for the Noongars (Daw et al, 2011; Greenskills, n.d.).

Turkey Bush

Family Scrophulariaceae Juss.

Botanical Name *Eremophila deserti* (Benth.) Chinnock.

Other Common Names Dogwood, Turkeybush and Turkish Bush.

Noongar Name Not known.

Field Notes Turkey Bush is a spreading shrub that grows to 4 m in height. It has long, green, lanceolate leaves and small white or cream flowers that appear in January (Birak) or from April to November (Djeran to Kambarang). Its fruits are ovoid berries (karlburi) that are yellow when ripe. This shrub grows quite prolifically around Geraldton and in the drier areas of Noongar country and along the coast around Esperance (FloraBase, 2018). It is also found in South Australia, Victoria, New South Wales and Queensland (Atlas of Living Australia, 2018).

Culinary Uses The ripe fruit of the Turkey Bush is reported to be edible and quite sweet to taste (Cribb and Cribb, 1974).

Botanical Name *Thysanotus patersonii* R.Br.

Other Common Name Twining Fringed Lily.

Noongar Names Tjunguri (South East Regional Centre for Urban Land Care, 2014) and Tjungoori (Meagher, 1975).

Field Notes Twining Fringe Lily, as the name suggests, is a twining, leafless, perennial, climbing plant with tuberous roots. It grows to around 1 m in height. Its purple flowers have three large, fringed petals and three smaller ones in between. It flowers from July to November (late Makuru to Kambarang). Twining Fringe Lily grows all over the south-west corner of Western Australia from Shark Bay to Esperance (FloraBase, 2018). It is also found in South Australia, New South Wales, Victoria and Tasmania (Atlas of Living Australia, 2018).

Family Asparagaceae Juss.

Culinary Uses The tubers of Twining Fringe Lily were eaten either raw or roasted in hot ashes (De Angeles, 2005; Low, 1991; SERCUL, 2014). The flowers and stems are also edible. The traditional way of eating these was to roll them into a ball that was then cooked in hot ashes for about ten to fifteen minutes, then ground to powder, then eaten with the root (bwoor) of the York Gum (*Eucalyptus loxophleba*) (Daw et al, 2011; Meagher, 1975).

There are two plants in the south-west of Western Australia called Veined Peppercress. They are both of the same family and both have edible leaves (Coppin, 2008).

Botanical Names *Lepidium rotundum* (Desv.) DC. and *Lepidium phlebopetalum* (F.Muell.) F.Muell.

Noongar Names Not known.

Field Notes *Lepidium rotundum* grows as either an erect or spreading shrub to under 1 m in height. It has long, slightly ovate, green leaves and white flowers with four petals that appear from July to November (late Makuru to Kambarang). This plant is mainly found in the south-west of Western Australia from Shark Bay to Esperance and in South Australia (Atlas of Living Australia, 2018; FloraBase, 2018). *Lepidium phlebopetalum* is a prostrate or erect annual or perennial plant that only grows to 0.3 m in height. It has wide, ovate

Family Brassicaceae Burnett

leaves and white flowers with a purple tinge that appear from May to September (late Djeran to Djilba). This plant is found in the drier regions of the southern half of Australia (Atlas of Living Australia, 2018).

Culinary Uses All plants of the *Lepidium* species are supposed to have edible leaves and stems and were eaten steamed (Coppin, 2008; Low, 1991).

Family Dioscoreaceae R.Br.

Botanical Name *Dioscorea hastifolia* Endl.

Other Common Name Native Yam.

Noongar Names Worrain, Warran, Warryn, Dtjokoh (Meagher, 1975), Warrany (Wheatbelt NRM, n.d.) and Woorine (SWALSC, 2016).

Field Notes Warrine is a perennial, scrambling or climbing tuberous shrub with stems growing up to 2 m in length. It has long, lanceolate, deeply veined, green leaves and small, yellow flowers that appear in a spike between May and July (Djeran and Makuru). The tuber of this plant can be quite long with some reported to be up to 2 m in length. Grey (1841), on his exploration of parts of the south-west, wrote of coming across plantations of what he thought were Warrine. This plant is endemic to Western Australia and is found from Shark Bay along the sandplains to Perth (FloraBase, 2018).

Culinary Uses Meagher (1975) wrote: 'This plant, which was called Worrain, has a long tuber which grows to a considerable depth (i.e. about 2 metres) and was dug up with a digging stick. It was cooked in the ashes and pounded before being eaten.' The tubers of this plant were a very important food source for the Noongars around Perth and to the north (Coppin, 2008; Daw et al, 2011; Gott, 2015; Maiden, 1889; Moore, 1884b).

Botanical Name *Persicaria hydropiper* (L.) Delarbre.

Other Common Names Marshpepper Knotweed, Marshpepper Smartweed, Redleaf and Smartweed.

Noongar Name Not known.

Field Notes Water Pepper is an erect, perennial herb that grows to 1.5 m in height and to 1.5 m in width. It has green or red lanceolate leaves that grow to around 10 cm long and small white flowers that appear in Western Australia in April (early Djeran) or December (early Birak). Water Pepper is endemic to the south-west of Western Australia and is found in damp areas near the coast from Lancelin to Albany (FloraBase, 2018). It is also found in South Australia, Queensland, New South Wales, Victoria, Tasmania and many other countries around the world (Atlas of Living Australia, 2018).

Family Polygonaceae Juss.

Culinary Uses Aboriginal groups around Australia ate the stems, which they roasted and peeled first (Taggart, n.d.).

Botanical Name *Cycnogeton huegelii* Endl. and *Cycnogeton lineare* (Endl.) Sond.

Other Common Names Swamp Arrowgrass and Creek Lily.

Noongar Name Not known.

Field Notes There are two species of Water Ribbons that grow in the south-west of Western Australia. They are rhizomatous plants that grow in water to 2 m in height. Both plants have long, slender, semi-erect or floating, ribbon-like leaves that arise from the base of the plant. The flower stalks can reach up to 30 cm in length. The plants flower during the warmer months (Kambarang to Bunuru). *Cycnogeton huegelii* is only found in water courses in Western Australia from Cervantes to Albany. *Cycnogeton lineare* is only found in the south-west of Western Australia from Cervantes to Esperance (Atlas of Living Australia, 2018).

Culinary Uses The starchy tubers of Water Ribbons were eaten raw or roasted in hot ashes. The roasted tubers ground up made good food for babies or the elderly (Bindon and Walley, 1992; Coppin, 2008).

Family Juncaginaceae Rich.

Cycnogeton huegelii

Weeping Pittosporum

Botanical Name *Pittosporum angustifolium* Lodd., G.Lodd & W.Lodd., also known as *Pittosporum phillyreoides*.

Other Common Names Butterbush, Native Willow, Poison Berry Tree, Gumbi Gumbi, Cattle Bush and Native Apricot (Lassak and McCarthy, 2008).

Noongar Name Wongin.

Field Notes Weeping Pittosporum grows as a weeping shrub or tree to around 8 m in height. The leaves vary in shape from ovate to elliptical and grow to 85 mm in length. The white or cream, bell-shaped flowers appear from June to October (Makuru to early Kambarang). The flowers are followed by smooth, yellow to orange fruit about 10 to 15 mm long (Cribb and Cribb, 1981; FloraBase, 2018). Weeping Pittosporum occurs from the Geraldton area along the coast to Perth then inland across the southern part of the state. It also

Family Pittosporaceae R.Br.

grows on Rottnest (Wadjemup), Garden Island (Meeandip) and Penguin Island (FloraBase, 2018; Rippey and Rowland, 1995). Weeping Pittosporum is found in all other Australian states and territories except Tasmania (Atlas of Living Australia, 2018).

Culinary Uses The seeds of the Weeping Pittosporum tree are edible and were ground into flour to make damper (mereny) by some groups. The seeds are reported to taste a bit bitter (Cribb and Cribb, 1974; Gott, 2010; Low, 1991; Maiden, 1889). The tree is reported to have a 'good, edible gum' (Cribb and Cribb, 1974).

Other Uses Parts of Weeping Pittosporum have medicinal properties. Infusions of the seeds, fruit pulp, leaves or wood, made by soaking the plant matter in water, were taken internally for the relief of pain and cramps. Decoctions (teas) made with the fruit pulp were drunk and applied externally for eczema and pruritus. Lassak and McCarthy (2008) warn that infusions and decoctions of this plant should not be taken too frequently as the 'haemolytic saponin present may prove injurious'. Compresses of warmed leaves of Weeping Pittosporum were placed on the breasts of new mothers to induce the flow of milk (Peile, 1997).

Family Chenopodiaceae Vent.

Botanical Name *Tecticornia lepidosperma* (Paul G.Wilson) K.A.Sheph. & Paul G.Wilson., also known as *Halosarcia lepidosperma*.

Other Common Names Sea Asparagus, Swamp Grass, Glasswort, Pickleweed and Sea Beans.

Noongar Name Milyu is the generic Noongar word for Samphire (Moore, 1884; Parks and Wildlife Service, 2018).

Field Notes Western Australian Samphire is a succulent plant that grows to around 1.3 m in both height and spread. Its light green stems are beaded from end to end. It is found in coastal and inland saline areas and on tidal mud flats (FloraBase, 2018). Western Australian Samphire only grows in the south-west of Western Australia and the very south of South Australia (Atlas of Living Australia, 2018).

Culinary Uses The beaded stems of this plant are edible. They can be eaten raw or steamed and are reported to taste slightly salty. It is best picked in summer and the young green shoots are reported to be the best eating (Tucker Bush, 2017).

Botanical Name *Linum marginale* Planch.

Other Common Name Native Flax.

Noongar Name Not known.

Field Notes Wild Flax is an erect, slender plant that grows to 1 m in height. It has a thick, tuberous rootstock and narrow leaves up to 20 mm long that taper to a soft point. Bright or pale blue or white flowers with five rounded petals appear in loose clusters at the top of the stalks and can be present most of the year, but peak flowering is from October to January (Kambarang to Birak) (Greening Australia, n.d.). In Western Australia Wild Flax is found growing in coastal and near-coastal habitats from Geraldton to Israelite Bay (FloraBase, 2018). It is also found in South Australia, Victoria, Tasmania, New South Wales and Southern Queensland (Atlas of Living Australia, 2018).

Family Linaceae Perleb.

Culinary Uses The oily seeds and stems of Wild Flax are edible and made a nice snack for Indigenous groups in the southern reaches of Australia (Cribb and Cribb, 1974; De Angeles, 2005; Gott, 2010; Maiden, 1889).

Other Uses The stems, when stripped and beaten to free the fibre, made good string (Gott, 2010).

Botanical Name *Pelargonium australe* Willd.

Other Common Name Native Storksbill.

Noongar Name Not known.

Field Notes Wild Geranium is a small plant that grows to 50 cm in height. The stems and leaves are hairy. Its leaves are ovate and lobed. Its flowers are white or pink with red streaks. They appear in groups of up to twelve flowers along the stalks from February to May (Bunuru to Djeran) or from September to December (late Djilba to early Birak) (Australian Native Plants Society (Australia), 2018; FloraBase, 2018). In Western Australia it is found in semi-arid areas and along the coast from Cervantes to Esperance. It is also found in South Australia, Victoria, Tasmania, New South Wales and southern Queensland (Atlas of Living Australia, 2018).

Family Geraniaceae Juss.

Culinary Uses The taproot of Wild Geranium is edible and was eaten roasted in hot ashes by Indigenous groups across the southern half of Australia including the Noongars of the south-west of Western Australia (Low, 1991).

Family Vitaceae Juss.

Botanical Name *Clematicissus angustissima* (F.Muell.) Planch.

Noongar Name Not known.

Field Notes Wild Grape is a scrambling or twining perennial climber that grows to around 3 m in height. Its small, green-yellow flowers have five petals. They appear from January to May (late Birak to late Djeran). Its globular fruits are dark purple when ripe (Leyland, 2002). Wild Grape is only found in Western Australia from Shark Bay along the Geraldton Sandplains to the Avon Wheatbelt (FloraBase, 2017).

Culinary Uses Noongars ate the fruit fresh or they dried them for later use. The leaves and young shoots are also edible and were eaten to prevent scurvy (Leyland, 2002). The roots can also be eaten but must be cooked for a long while before eating (Naughtin, 2018).

Wild Plum

Botanical Name *Podocarpus drouynianus* F.Muell.

Other Common Names Emu Plum and Emu Berry.

Noongar Name Koolah (Abbott, 1983; Daw et al, 2011; Meagher, 1974; SERCUL, 2014) and Quondan (Bindon and Chadwick, 1992).

Field Notes Wild Plum is related to the conifers and grows as a small to medium shrub up to 3 m in height. It is multi-stemmed and can spread to a few metres across. It has male and female parts on separate plants. It has thin, needle-like leaves and small yellow flowers that appear on spikes from August to December (Djilba to Birak). The fruit (or female cone) of the Wild Plum is really a seed with a fleshy covering that looks like a plum. This tree is endemic to the south-west of Western Australia only. There are small areas of this tree around Perth, but most are found on the south coast from

Family Podocarpaceae Endl.

Busselton to Albany (FloraBase, 2018; SERCUL, 2014).

Culinary Uses The large fruit of Wild Plum was a nutritious dietary supplement for Noongars but is reported to be a bit bland (Coppin, 2008; Daw et al, 2011; SERCUL, 2014).

Wireleaf Mistletoe

Botanical Name *Amyema preissii* (Miq.) Tiegh.

Noongar Name Nyilla Nyilla (the generic Noongar name for mistletoe).

Field Notes Wireleaf Mistletoe is a climbing, hemiparasitic plant that is usually found growing on Acacia, but occasionally on other trees. It has green, needle-like leaves that are up to 8 cm in length and 2 mm in width. Its red-orange, tubular flowers that grow up to 26 mm in length can be present all year round (FloraBase, 2018). Its white or pink, translucent fruits are globose and are 8 to 10 mm in diameter. Wireleaf Mistletoe is native to most of Western Australia but is also found in all other mainland states of Australia (Atlas of Living Australia, 2018).

Culinary Uses The fruits of the Wireleaf Mistletoe are edible when ripe (Cribb and Cribb, 1987).

Family Loranthaceae Juss.

Woody Pear

Botanical Name *Xylomelum occidentale* R.Br.

Noongar Names Dumbung, Janjin (Moore, 1842), Danja, Koongal (Abbott, 1983), Quabba and Kogala (Nannup, N., in discussion with the author, July 2018).

Field Notes Woody Pear grows as a small, twisted shrub or tree from 2 to 8 m in height. It has dark, flaky bark and oak-like leaves. The fruit of the Woody Pear, as the name suggests, is pear-shaped with a large woody seed. Long, creamy-white, spikey flowers appear in clumps at the end of branchlets from December to February (Birak to early Bunuru) (FloraBase, 2018; Forest Products Commission Western Australia, n.d.). Woody Pear is endemic to Western Australia and is only found in a small area of the south-west, near the coast, from Yanchep to Augusta (FloraBase, 2018).

Family Proteaceae Juss.

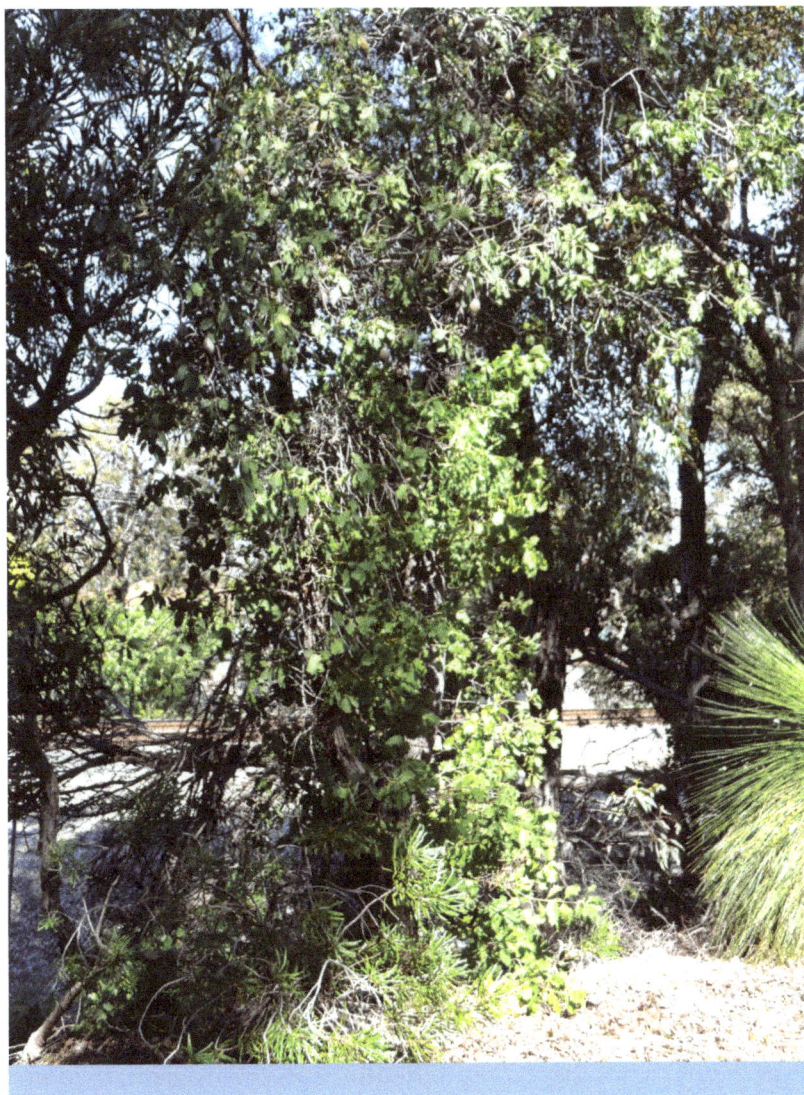

Culinary Uses The kernel in the seed of Woody Pear can be roasted and eaten (Hansen and Horsfall, 2016).

Other Uses Infusions of the crushed leaves and bark (boort), made by soaking the plant matter in water, were taken internally for pain relief (Lassak and McCarthy, 2008).

Family Asteraceae Bercht. & J.Presl

Botanical Name *Microseris walteri* Gand., also known as *Microseris scapigera,* and *Microseris forsteri.*

Other Common Names Murnong, Yam Daisy, Native Yam, Black Fellows Yam and Native Dandelion.

Noongar Name Woorine (SWALSC, 2017).

Field Notes The Yam is an erect, tuberous perennial plant that grows to around 80 cm in height. It lies dormant in summer and springs to life again in autumn. It has long, ovate, green leaves that grow from the base, and yellow, daisy-like flowers that have many petals. The flowers appear from September to October (late Djilba to early Kambarang). In Western Australia, the Yam is found in the south-west from Albany to Esperance and around the Goldfields and Eastern Mallee (FloraBase, 2018). It is also found in South Australia, Victoria, Tasmania and New South Wales (Atlas of Living Australia, 2018).

Culinary Uses Before settlement by Europeans, the tubers of the Yam were extensively cultivated and enjoyed raw or roasted in hot ashes, or steamed in an earth oven, by Indigenous groups right across the southern reaches of Australia. The tubers are reported to taste a bit like radish (Cribb and Cribb, 1974; Gott, 2010; Low, 1991; Maiden 1889; Pascoe, 2014). In some parts of Australia, the plant has been eaten almost to extinction by sheep (Gott, 2010; Pascoe, 2014).

Family Hypoxidaceae R.Br.

Botanical Name *Pauridia vaginata* (Schltdl.) Snijman & Kocyan., formerly known as *Hypoxis vaginata*.

Noongar Name Not known.

Field Notes Yellow Star is a small herb that grows to around 35 cm in height. Its roots are swollen corms that are less than 2 cm long. Its long, thin, flat leaves grow from the base to 35 cm in length. Its flowers are yellow and star-like with six petals. The plant favours water-logged ground (Gott, 2010; Royal Botanic Gardens Victoria, 2015). In Western Australia this plant is found in isolated coastal and near-coastal patches from Perth to Esperance (FloraBase, 2018). It is also found in South Australia, Victoria and Tasmania (Atlas of Living Australia, 2018).

Culinary Uses The roots (bwoor) of Yellow Star are edible and Noongars ate them after roasting them in hot ashes (Gott, 2010).

Botanical Name *Platysace deflexa* (Turcz.) C.Norman.

Other Common Name Ravensthorpe Radish.

Noongar Names Youcka (Hassell, 1975), Youlk and Yug.

Field Notes Youlk is a tuberous, perennial shrub that grows to 1 m in height. It has small, green, ovate leaves and white, star-shaped flowers with five petals that appear at any time of the year. It is endemic to a small part of Western Australia from the Avon Wheatbelt to Albany and Esperance (FloraBase, 2018).

Culinary Uses The tubers of Youlk are quite large and look like Nadine or Kipfler potatoes that you buy in the supermarket. Noongars south of Perth ate these tubers raw or

roasted in hot ashes. There are moves afoot to cultivate these commercially in Western Australia (Fawcett, 2014; Woodall et al, 2009).

Family Zamiaceae Horan.

Botanical Names There are two Zamias that are endemic to the south-west of Western Australia: one just called Zamia (*Macrozamia riedlei* (Gaudich.) C.A.Gardner) and Sandplain Zamia (*Macrozamia fraseri* Miq.).

Other Common Name Zamia Palm.

Noongar Names Biana *(Macrozamia riedlei)* (Bindon and Chadwick, 1992), Quinnin (Hassell, 1975), Jeeriji (SERCUL, 2014; Daw et al, 2011) and Djiridj (Wheatbelt NRM, 2015). The Zamia nuts were known as Baio, Bayio, Boyoo (Meagher, 1975) and Kwinin (Moore, 1884b). The pulp of the nut was called Byyu (Meagher, 1975) and Dyundo (Moore, 1842).

Field Notes Zamias are cycads, usually trunkless, that grow to 3 m in height. Cycads are very old plants that have been around for over 200 million years (PlantNET, 2018). The leaves of Zamias are glossy, and either flat or openly keeled.

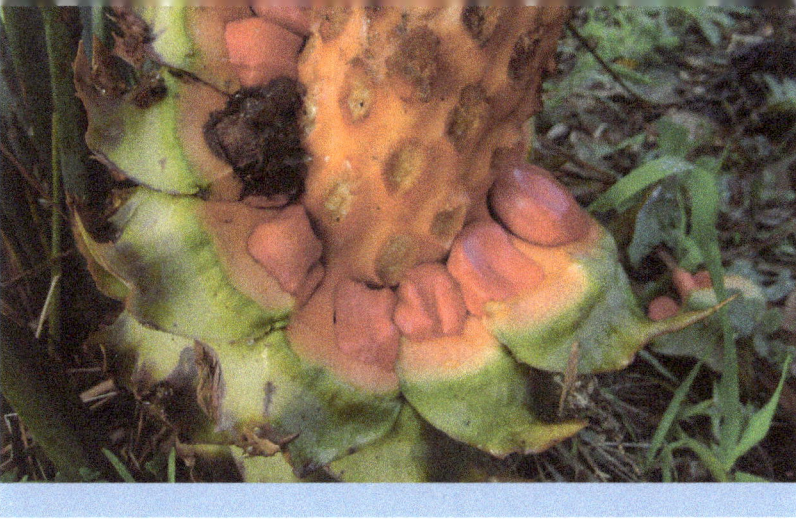

Their seed cones are ovoid, up to 35 cm long and 18 cm in diameter. Zamias (*Macrozamia riedlei*) are found in abundance in coastal and near-coastal habitats from Perth to Albany. Sandplain Zamias (*Macrozamia fraseri*) are more confined to an area from Geraldton to Bunbury (FloraBase, 2018).

Culinary Uses The seeds of both Zamias are toxic unless treated to remove the toxins. Many early settlers became violently ill after eating untreated seeds. The various Noongar dialect groups had different ways of removing the toxins. Some would bury the seeds for up to six months then soak them in water for a few days; others would soak them in water first then bury them for a while. After treatment some groups would only eat the skin of the seeds while other groups would crush the seeds into a pulp, shape the pulp into cakes and then roast the cakes in hot ashes. The seeds are reported to taste a bit like tomatoes (City of Joondalup, 2011; Daw et al, 2011; Low, 1991; Meagher, 1975).

Other Uses Noongars ground the raw seeds into a powder and threw the powder into rivers or streams to stun the fish and make them easier to catch. Noongars also used the woolly material found around the base of the fronds as fire tinder, or as an absorbent material for personal hygienic purposes (SERCUL, 2014).

Fungi (Woorda or Noomar)

George Grey (1841) reported in his journal that he'd seen seven species of fungi eaten by the Western Australian Aborigines. He commented that, 'The different kinds of fungus are very good. In certain seasons of the year they are abundant, and the natives eat them greedily.' On the following pages are examples of edible fungi (woorda or noomar) that are indigenous to Noongar country; that is, the south-west corner of Western Australia.

Caution

A licence is needed to collect fungi on Crown land in Western Australia. People collecting wild fungi to eat need to check with a fungi expert before eating wild mushrooms as there are poisonous look-alikes that can cause death if eaten.

Shaggy Ink Cap (*Coprinus comatus*)

Beefsteak Fungus

Scientific Name *Fistulina hepatica* (Schaeff.) With.

Noongar Name Nornarr.

Field Notes Beefsteak Fungus is so named because it looks like a piece of raw steak when young. It is parasitic on living and rotting trees. It is common in coastal and near coastal habitats from Perth to Albany. It is also found in South Australia, Victoria, Tasmania, New South Wales and in the southern reaches of Queensland (Atlas of Living Australia, 2018).

Culinary Uses Beefsteak Fungus was eaten by Western Australian Indigenous groups (Fungimap, n.d.).

Family Fistulinaceae Lotsy

Family Pluteaceae Kotl. & Pouzar

Scientific Name *Volvopluteus gloiocephalus* (DC.) Vizzini, Contu & Justo.

Other Common Names Pink-gilled Volvariella, Big Sheath Mushroom, Rose-gilled Grisette and Stubble Rosegill.

Noongar Name Not known.

Field Notes The Common Rosegill is a mushroom that has a conical body with pink gills underneath. Stems have been seen up to 20 cm in length. The cap is white to greyish in colour, slimy when fresh but drying later (Fungimap, n.d; Kuo, 2004). This mushroom commonly appears after the first rains in autumn (late Bunuru and Djeran). The Common Rosegill is found in the more temperate areas of Australia (Atlas of Living Australia, 2018) and on most other continents.

Culinary Uses The Common Rosegill is edible and is best cooked in soups and casseroles (Fungimap, n.d.).

Scientific Name *Ramaria capitata* (Lloyd) Corner (1950).

Noongar Name Not known.

Field Notes The Coral Fungus looks like a piece of coral, hence the name. It grows to around 7 cm in height and is salmon coloured. It grows along the south coast of Western Australia from Augusta to Albany. It is also found along the south coast of Queensland, parts of the New South Wales and Victorian coasts and all over Tasmania (Cribb and Cribb, 1987).

Culinary Uses The Coral Fungus is edible (Cribb and Cribb, 1987).

Family Gomphaceae Donk.

Dog Poo Fungus

Family Sclerodermaceae Corda.

Scientific Name *Pisolithus* Sp.

Other Common Names Horse Dung Fungus, Dead Man's Foot, Puffballs and Earth Balls.

Noongar Name Dwert Goona Noomar (Nannup, N., in discussion with the author, July 2018).

Field Notes The Dog Poo Fungus and other fungi of this species appear as common brown puffballs, pale to dark mottled brown in colour. They can grow up to 20 cm in diameter and 20 cm in height. As they age the puffballs break down into a mass of powdery spores (Bougher, 2009; Leithhead, n.d.). Dog Poo Fungi are very common in disturbed leaf litter, especially around Eucalypts. They are found throughout Australia and are indigenous to and very common in the south-west of Western Australia. They are also found worldwide (Readford, 2011).

Culinary Uses The young fruits of Dog Poo Fungi can be eaten but Noongars only ate them when food was scarce (Australian National Botanic Gardens, 2018).

Other Uses Dog Poo Fungi have medicinal properties. The fruits were broken open and the spores were rubbed into wounds and sores to prevent infection and promote healing. According to Robinson (2007a), 'the fresh firm fruits of this species were once used in some European countries to make a khaki dye for military uniforms'.

Family Agaricaceae Chevall.

Scientific Name *Agaricus campestris* L.

Noongar Name Not known.

Field Notes The common Field Mushroom has a white cap growing to 10 centimetres in diameter. When young they are a rounded shape before they flatten out with maturity. The gills underneath are initially pink but darken as the mushroom ages. Their stalks can be up to 10 cm in length. The Field Mushroom is usually seen after the first rains in autumn (Bunuru and Djeran) (First Nature, 2018). In Western Australia they are found in woodlands and grassy areas from Perth to Albany. They are also found in all other Australian states and territories and in many other countries (Atlas of Living Australia, 2018).

Culinary Uses The Field Mushroom is edible (Cole, 2012; Cribb and Cribb, 1974).

Scientific Name *Agaricus langei* (F.H.Møller) F.H.Møller.

Other Common Name Scaly Wood Mushroom.

Noongar Name Not known.

Field Notes The Forest Mushroom's cap grows to 12 cm in diameter with a stem of up to 12 cm in length. The cap is convex and densely covered in fine rust-brown scales. Its flesh is whitish with a pink tinge. Its gills are a pale pink at first then becoming darker with age. It tastes and smells pleasant and mushroomy. The Forest Mushroom appears in woodlands around Perth in late summer and autumn (Bunuru and Djeran). It is also found in Victoria and in other countries such as the United Kingdom (Rogers Mushrooms, 2016).

Culinary Uses Forest Mushrooms are edible (Low, 1991).

Family Agaricaceae Chevall.

Family **Polyporaceae** Fr. ex Corda.

Scientific Name *Laccocephalum mylittae* (Cooke & Massee) Núñez & Ryvarden.

Noongar Name Metup (Bindon and Chadwick, 1992).

Field Notes The Native Bread fungus has a large fruiting body than can be up to 20 cm or more in diameter and flat or dome-shaped with a white spore layer underneath. It is a wood-decay fungus, but the fruit body develops from a large underground organ called a sclerotium. This fungus appears after bushfires in Eucalypt forests around the coast from Perth to Albany (Robinson, 2007b). It is also found near the coast in Southern Queensland, New South Wales, Victoria and Tasmania (Atlas of Living Australia, 2018).

Culinary Uses This fungus is edible (Cribb and Cribb, 1974; Lepp, 2012; Fungimap, n.d.; Maiden, 1889). Robinson (2007b) relates that, 'Europeans recorded Aboriginal people

searching for the underground sclerotia, which they ate either raw or cooked.'

Scientific Name *Choiromyces aboriginum* Trappe.

Noongar Name Not known.

Field Notes Native Truffle is a truffle-like fungus that is roughly spherical in shape and grows to about 7 cm in diameter. Noongars looking for this fungus would look for the cracks in the overlying soils where the fungus was trying to push through. Native Truffle is found in the dry areas of Western Australia, South Australia and the Northern Territory (Lepp, 2012).

Culinary Uses Lepp (2012) reports that, 'It [Native Truffle] is a traditional native food and has also been used as a source of water.' The fruiting bodies were eaten raw or cooked briefly in hot ashes.

Family Tuberaceae Dumort.

Scientific Name *Coprinus comatus* (O.F.Müll.) Pers.

Other Common Names Lawyer's Wig and Shaggy Mane.

Noongar Name Not known.

Field Notes Shaggy Ink Cap has a tall, cylindrical, whitish cap covered in brown-tipped white scales that sits atop a white stem up to 15 cm in height. The gills start out cream, turning pale brown, then very quickly blackening and liquifying to a slimy patch, hence the name (Cribb and Cribb, 1987). It is common in the south-west of Western Australia from Perth to Esperance and is also found in South Australia, Victoria, New South Wales, southern Queensland and Tasmania (Atlas of Living Australia, 2018).

Culinary Uses The Shaggy Ink Cap is reported to be edible if collected and eaten before it starts to collapse (Cribb and Cribb, 1987).

Family Agaricaceae Chevall.

Family Agaricaceae Chevall.

Scientific Name *Chlorophyllum rhacodes* (Vittad.) Vellinga, also known as *Macrolepiota rhacodes*.

Noongar Name Not known.

Field Notes The Shaggy Parasol Mushroom has a distinctly scaly, white to cream cap at first that turns brown as it ages. The cap can grow to 15 cm in diameter. The cap starts off ovate then flattens out as it grows bigger. The stem is bulbous at its base. The spores can be white, cream or yellowish in colour. It grows on the ground in woodlands in the south-west of Western Australia and Victoria. It is also found in many other countries including the United Kingdom and North America (Kuo, 2015; Rogers Mushrooms, 2016).

Culinary Uses The Shaggy Parasol Mushroom is edible and is reported to have a pleasant flavour (Cole, 2012; Cribb and Cribb, 1974; Rogers Mushrooms, 2016).

Noongar Vocabulary

From Bindon and Chadwick, 1992

English	Noongar
ashes	yuwart
bad (unfit to eat)	wockun
bag	cout, goto, kooda, kooda-kooda, coorda, kooter
bark (of a tree)	boort, janny, djanne, yabbul, bunner morba
berry (general)	kwolberi, yet yet, yurenburt
berry (red and sweet)	mol
berry (sweet)	kurup
branch (of a tree)	boorn
bury (verb – to put in the ground)	danbar (danbar ejoween)
bush country	nganjima
bush (general)	barang, marlak
bush with medicinal properties	kurin
carry in a bag	gotang, kotang
carry or bring (verb – to carry or bring)	ganga, gangow
carrying dish	djildjit, milkoorn, yandi
charcoal	yarrkal, kob, bidil, kallabidyl, murhro, kup, yargyl, bedyle, kalaeenak, kalaee-nytch
chew (verb – to chew)	daturnungur
chewing	goolangeen
clean (verb – to clean)	elungur
coals or embers	bridal, kalla inak
cook (verb – to cook)	dukun, dookern, dookarn, tokoon, dookkoon, bedarung

English	Noongar
cooked (sufficient for eating)	djidik, kannar, dookooner, djeedara
cooking	dookerniny
crook (stick for pulling down Banksia flowers)	kalga
crush (verb – to crush)	coolyarn
cut (verb – to cut)	deidung, bornungan, karjut
damper (bread)	mandjarli, marrin , mereny, quannert
dig (verb – to dig)	bingur, bean, bingun, plangur, bian
dig out of the ground (verb)	denburingh
digging	biyaniny
digging stick (men)	waan
digging stick (women)	wanna, warna
dough	merindjook, merinyook
drink (verb – to drink)	marlyeril, nganign, nalcutin, kodo woorong
dry (verb – to make dry)	injarun, jadam
eat (verb – to eat)	angur, ngannow, nan-gur, ngalkoo, ngan
eating	djoriny
fire	gyala, kaal, kahla, karla, kaarl
firestick	kalamarta
fire wood	kaarl boorn, bounuh
flame of the fire	kalla dalla, kata djallup
flour	mereny, djari, djookoot
flower (blossom)	booneat
foliage	myaree
food (animal and vegetable)	dadjamaryn

English	Noongar
forest	djarilmari, marlak
fruit	koolah, wootah, jiljee
fungus (general)	woorda, noomar
gathering fruits and berries	merany barang
grain	kwolak
grass (general)	djiraly
grinding stone	mullers, kodja, tabba
gum (edible)	djoolbar, djunbar
gum of the Grass Tree (Balga)	perin, nargalya, nallang, tudibi, biriny, mirlen, kadjo, pining, peenck
gum of a Wattle Tree	kalyang
hungry	eulub, bandyne, bordunyuk, yoolup
knife	darp, taap, tabba, dabba, bondjun, boondura
leaf, a gum-leaf	balgore
mixing	wirdanginy
mouldy	menudo, minyudo
nectar (general)	ngonyang
nectar (from Banksias)	djidja
nectar drink (made by soaking flowers in water)	jjilyaa, mangite, mungitch
nectar drink after fermenting	gep
palatable	mulyit mulyit
plenty	boorlarang, boola
pound (verb – to pound)	kolyurang
pounding (of roots before eating)	bedangweenun
put (verb – to put in a bag)	durrungur

English	Noongar
putrid	badjark
quartz for fire lighting	bilying, borryl, bardya
resin (Grasstree)	biriny
rock (pestle for grinding stone)	boye
root (of a tree)	malle, malla, bwoor, baynyer
salt	djallum
sap (generic term)	mayat
sap (from a Redgum tree)	ngarl
skin bag	kutj, bwokoot, kooda, gotang, durrungur
steep (verb - to soak in water)	nugoolung, nyogulang
stone axe	kotj, kwetj, kodja
stone knife	daap, boondura
swallow (verb - to swallow)	ngannow
sweet	kaling-ween, mooyit mooyit, guabamet, ngocolmocol, mulyi mulyi, knootabata, ngugo, mingithe, dunatch, ngungang, ngok, mundange, mindanga, mangite, koortboola, bundegooer, quonotook, ngueinch
taste (verb - to taste)	pacanan, pacianaco, pacianana
thirsty (wanting water)	gabby goorduk, kabigoordak
unpalatable	djool
vegetable food (all plants, parts of which are eaten)	maryn
water	kabi, kep, kuypa, kuyp, gabby
water (fresh)	gabby djekoo
zamia nut/seed	baio, bayio, boyoo, kwinin

References

Abbott, I. (1983). *Aboriginal Names for Plant Species in South-Western Australia*. Technical Paper No 5. Forests Department of Western Australia.

Apace WA. (n.d.a). *Solanum symonii*. www.apacewa.org.au/plants/view/239/Solanum-symonii/catalogue:3

Apace WA. (n.d.b). *Bush Tucker Plants for your Garden*. www.apacewa.org.au/wp-content/uploads/2016/09/Bush-Tucker-species-descriptions.pdf

Archer, W. (2018). *Esperance Wildflowers*. www.esperancewildflowers.blogspot.com.au

Atlas of Living Australia. (2018). www.ala.org.au

Australian Geographic. (n.d.). *Guide to Australia's Gum Blossoms*. www.australiangeographic.com.au/topics/science-environment/2010/04/guide-to-australias-gum-blossoms/

Australian National Botanic Gardens. (2011). *Aboriginal Trail*. www.anbg.gov.au/gardens/visiting/exploring/aboriginal-trail/

Australian National Botanic Gardens. (2012). *Aboriginal Plant Use in SE Australia*. www.anbg.gov.au/aborig.s.e.aust/s.e.a.mapkey.html

Australian National Botanic Gardens, (2013). *Australian Fungi*. www.anbg.gov.au/fungi/aboriginal.html.

Australian National Botanic Gardens. (2018). www.anbg.gov.au.

Australian Native Nursery. (n.d.). Current Plant List. www.australiannativenursery.com.au/wp-content/uploads/2016/05/currentplantlist.pdf.

Australian Native Plants Society (Australia). (2018). www.anpsa.org.au.

Australian Plants Online. (2003). *Santalum – A Fascinating Genus*. www.anpsa.org.au/APOL31/sep03-3.html

Australian Plants Society, S.A. Inc. (2018). *Bush Tucker*. www.australianplantssa.asn.au/pages/australian-plants/general-articles/bush-tucker.php

Barrett, R. and E. Tay. (2016). *Perth Plants: A Field Guide to the Bushland and Coastal Flora of Kings Park and Bold Park*. Perth: CSIRO Publishing.

Bennett, E. M., (1991). *Common and Aboriginal Names of Western Australian Plant Species*. Perth: Wildflower Association of Western Australia.

Bindon, P. (1996). *Useful Bush Plants*. Perth: Western Australian Museum.

Bindon, P. and R. Chadwick. (1992). A *Nyoongar Word List from the South-West of Western Australia*. Perth: Western Australian Museum.

Bindon, P. and T. Walley. (1992). Hunters and Gatherers. *Landscope*, vol. 8, no. 1.

Birdlife Australia. (n.d.). *Choosing Plants for Black-Cockatoos*. geocatch.asn.au/wp-content/uploads/2018/04/Choosing-Plants-for-Black-Cockatoos.pdf

Bouger, N. (2009). *Fungi of the Perth Region and Beyond*. www.fungiperth. org.au/Download-document/82-Field-Book-Part.html

Bradshaw Foundation. (2011). *Journey of Mankind*. www.bradshawfoundation. com/stephenoppenheimer/index.php

Brigs, B. (n.d.) *Typha Domingensis*. www.anbg.gov.au/abrs/online-resources/ flora/stddisplay.xsql?pnid=57504

Cambridge Coast Care. (n.d.). *Plants of the West Coast: Acrotriche cordata - Coastal Blueberry*. www.cambridgecoastcare.com.au/wp-content/ uploads/2015/05/P44_Acrotriche-cordata-COASTAL-BLUEBERRY.pdf

Chaffey, C. (2002). A Fern which Changed Australian History. *Australian Plants Online*. www.anpsa.org.au/APOL26/jun02-6.html

Cicada Woman Tours. (2013). *Plants Used by Aboriginal People*. www.cicadawoman.weebly.com/uploads/8/7/3/4/8734418/plants_used_ by_aboriginal_people_april_2013.pdf

City of Bayswater. (2010). *Local Native Plants Guide*. www.bayswater.wa.gov. au/cproot/926/2/local-native-plants-2016.pdf

City of Charles Sturt. (n.d.). *Local coastal plants*. www.tennyson.org.au/assets/ gardens.pdf

City of Joondalup. (2011). *Plants and People in Mooro Country: Noongar Plant Use in Yellagonga Regional Park*. www.joondalup.wa.gov.au/Files/ Plants%20and%20People%20in%20Mooro%20Country.pdf

Clarke, A. (1985). Fruits and Seeds as Foods for Southern South Australian Aborigines. *Journal of the Anthropolical Society of South Australia*, vol. 23, no. 9, pp. 9-22.

Cole, M. (2012). *Edible or Poisonous Mushrooms? How to determine which is which*. www.agpath.com.au/wp/wp-content/uploads/2014/04/Permicul- ture-Baw-Baw-March-1st-2012.pdf

Coppin, P. (2008). *Nyoongar Food Plant Species*. www.petercoppin.com/ factsheets/edible/nyoongar.pdf.

Crago, J. (n.d.). *Scaevola Spinescens, (Maroon Bush, Murin Murin, Prickly Fan Flower, Current Bush)*. www.bushmedicine.ws/page6.html

Cribb, A. and J. Cribb. (1983). *Wild Medicine in Australia*. Sydney: Fontana Books.

Cribb, A. and J. Cribb. (1987). *Wild Food in Australia* (2nd edn). Sydney: Fontana/Collins.

Cunningham, I. (1998). *The Trees That Were Nature's Gift*. Maylands: The Environmental Printing Company.

Dann, D. (2003). *Waranygu: Digging for Food*. Geraldton: Yamaji Language Centre.

Davey, K. (2000). *Life on Australian Seashores*. www.mesa.edu.au/friends/seashores/h_banksii.html

Daw, B., T. Walley and G. Keighery. (2011). *Bush Tucker Plants of the South-West*. Kensington; Department of Environment and Conservation.

De Angeles, D. (2005). *Aboriginal Use Plants of the Greater Melbourne Area*. www.latrobe.edu.au/wildlife/downloads/Aboriginal-plant-use-list.pdf

Denmark Arts. (2005). *The Noongar Seasons and Food Cycle*. www.denmarkarts.com.au/documents/6seasons-info.doc

Department of Primary Industries, Parks, Water and Environment. (n.d.). *Threatened Flora of Tasmania: Atriplex suberecta*. www.naturalvalues-atlas.tas.gov.au/downloadattachment?id=13754

Dix, W. and S. Meagher. (1976). Fish Traps in the South West of Western Australia. *Records of the Western Australian Museum*, vol. 4, no. 2.

eFlora.SA. (2018). www.flora.sa.gov.au

Encyclopaedia Britannica. (2018). *Donkey Orchid*. www.britannica.com

Encyclopaedia of Life (EOL). (2018). www.eol.org

Euclid. (2018). *Eucalypts of Southern Australia*. www.anbg.gov.au/cpbr/cd-keys/Euclid/sample/html/index.htm

Explore Melville. (2012). *Bush tucker plants used by Aboriginals in the Perth area*. www.exploremelville.targeton.com/library/bush-tucker-plants/bush-tucker-plants

Fawcett, A. (2014). *RIG News - September 2014*. www.remoteindigenous-gardens.net/wp-content/uploads/RIG-News-SEPT-2014.pdf

Fern, K. (2018). *Capparis spinosa nummularia*. Tropical Plants Database. www.tropical.theferns.info/viewtropical.php?id=Capparis+spinosa+nummularia

First Nature. (2018). *Agaricus campestris L. - Field Mushroom*. www.first-nature.com/fungi/agaricus-campestris.php

Florabank. (2018). www.florabank.org.au

FloraBase. (2018). *The Western Australian Flora*. www.FloraBase.dec.wa.gov.au

Flora of Australia Online. (2018). www.environment.gov.au/science/abrs/online-resources/flora-of-australia-online

Flora NT (2017). *Northern Territory Flora Online*. www.eflora.nt.gov.au

Florek, S. (2014). *Food Culture: Aboriginal Bread*. www.australianmuseum.net.au/blogpost/science/food-culture-aboriginal-bread

Forest Products Commission Western Australia. (n.d.). *Woody Pear*. www.fpc.wa.gov.au/content_migration/plantations/species/native_forests/woody_pear.aspx

Frawley, W. (2004). *International Encyclopedia of Linguistics* (2nd edn). Melbourne: Oxford University Press.

French, M. (2012). *Eucalypts of Western Australia's Wheatbelt*. Padbury: Malcolm French.

Friends of the Queens Park Bushland. (2011). *Xanthorrhoea preissii*. www.friendsofqueensparkbushland.org.au/xanthorrhoea-preissii.

Fungimap. (n.d.). *Laccocephalum mylittae – Native Bread*. www.fungimap.org.au/index.php/fduonline-home/105/294/polypores/P-laccocephalum-mylittae

Fungimap. (n.d.). *Volvariella speciose – Common Rosegill*. www.fungimap.org.au/index.php/fduonline-home/159/294/agarics/P-volvariella-speciosa

Gohil, K., J. Patel and A. Gajjar. (2010). Pharmacological Review on Centella asiatica: A Potential Herbal Cure-all. *Indian Journal of Pharmaceutical Sciences*, vol. 72, no. 5, pp. 546–556.

Goode, B., J. Hohnen, C. Irvine and A. Tarbotton. (2010). *An Aboriginal Cultural Heritage Management Assessment For The Ellensbrook Catchment*. www.bradgoode.com.au/wp-content/uploads/2014/06/HERITAGE-MANAGEMENT-REPORT-DEC-ELLENSBROOK-FINAL-14092010.pdf

Goode, B., C. Irvine, J Harris & M. Thomas. (2005). *'Kinjarling' the Place of Rain: The City of Albany & Department of Indigenous Affairs Aboriginal Heritage Survey*. www.albany.wa.gov.au/Kinjarling_Heritage_Survery_Brad_Goode__Assoc_March_2005_RPT1280.pdf

Gott, B. (2010). *Aboriginal Plants in the Grounds of Monash University*. www.fsd.monash.edu.au/files/bethgottpamphlet_po.pdf

Gott, B. (2015). *Aboriginal Trail*. www.anbg.gov.au/gardens/visiting/exploring/aboriginal-trail/

Green, N. (1979). *Nyungar – the People*. www.kippleonline.net/bobhoward/Nind.html

Greening Australia. (n.d.). *Glycine tabacina*. www.jingeri.com/wp-content/uploads/2014/11/Glycine_tabacina.pdf

Greening Australia. (n.d.). *Linum marginale*. www.greeningaustralia.org.au/uploads/knowledge-portal/ACT_SPA_fact_sheet_Linum_marginale.pdf

Greenskills. (n.d.). *Plants of Denmark's Walk Trails: Traditional Noongar uses*. www.greenskills.org.au/pub/pamph/plants.pdf

Grey, G. (1840). *A vocabulary of the dialects of South-Western Australia.* London: T. and W. Boone.

Grey, G. (1841) *Journals of Two Expeditions of Discovery in North-West and Western Australia Volume II.* London: T. and W. Boone.

Griffiths, T. (ed.) (2009). Dornderup Wongie: *Noongar Language of the Southwest.* (Draft) www.academia.edu/8946957/Dornderup_Wongie_Noongar_Language_Dictionary_Wardandi_Nyungar_draft

Hansen, V. and J. Horsfall. (2016). *Noongar Bush Medicine: Medicinal Plants of the South-west of Western Australia.* Perth: UWA Publishing.

HerbiGuide. (2014). www.herbiguide.com.au

Hassell, E. (1975). *My Dusky Friends.* Dalkeith, WA: C. W. Hassell.

Herman, M. (2001). *Favourites – 5.* Australian Plants Online. www.anpsa.org.au/APOL22/jun01-9.html

Howard, R. (n.d.). *P. P. King's Noongar Word List (1821).* www.kippleonline.net/bobhoward/king.html

iNaturalist.org. (n.d.). *Ecklonia radiata.* www.inaturalist.org/guide_taxa/485255

iNaturalist.org. (n.d.). *Tassel Flower (Leucopogon verticillatus).* www.inaturalist.org/taxa/153108-Leucopogon-verticillatus

Indigenous Flora and Fauna Association. (n.d.). *Atriplex semibaccata.* www.iffa.org.au/atriplex-semibaccata.

Isaacs, J. (1992). *Bush Food: Aboriginal Food and Herbal Medicine.* Sydney: Ure Smith Press.

Kapitany, A. (2015) *Edible Succulent Plants.* www.australiansucculents.com/edible-succulents

Kuo, M. (2004). *Volvariella speciosa.* www.mushroomexpert.com/volvariella_speciosa.html

Kuo, M. (2015). *Chlorophyllum rhacodes.* www.mushroomexpert.com/chlorophyllum_rhacodes.html

Lassak, E. and T. McCarthy. (2008). *Australian Medicinal Plants.* Sydney: Read New Holland.

Leithhead, B. (n.d.). *Fungi Photos Group P, Phlebopus marginatus to Podoscypha petalodes.* www.elfram.com/fungi/fungipics_p.html

Lepp, H. (2012). *Aboriginal use of fungi.* www.anbg.gov.au/fungi/aboriginal.html

Leyland, E. (2002). *Wajarri Wisdom: Food and Medicinal Plants of the Mullewa/Murchison District of WA.* Geraldton: Yamaji Language Centre.

Lim, T. (2016). *Edible Medicinal and Non-medicinal Plants, Volume 11: Modified Stems, Roots Bulbs*. Switzerland: Springer International Publishing.

Low, T. (1991). *Wild Food Plants of Austalia*. Sydney: Harper Collins Publishers.

Lucid Key Server. (2015). *Sarcozona praecox*. www.keys.lucidcentral.org/ keys/v3/scotia/key/Plants%20and%20Fungi%20of%20south%20 western%20NSW/Media/Html/Sarcozona_praecox.htm

Maiden, J. (1889). *The Useful Native Plants of Australia*. Sydney: The Technological Museum of New South Wales.

Mary River Catchment Coordinating Committee. (2014). *A guide to some edible/useful (mostly) local species*. www.mrccc.org.au/wp-content/ uploads/2013/10/Edible-and-useful-native-plants.pdf

Meagher, S. (1974). The Food Resources of the Aborigines of the South-West of Western Australia. *Records of the Western Australian Museum*, vol. 3, 14-65.

Milkwood. (2016). *Foraging, Drying and Eating Seaweed in Australia*. www.milkwood.net/2016/06/06/foraging-drying-using-seaweed-australia/

Moore, G. (1884a). *A Descriptive Vocabulary of the Language in Common Use Amongst the Aborigines of Western Australia*. London: Orr.

Moore, G. (1884b). *Diary of Ten Years Eventful Life of an Early Settler in Western Australia*. London: M. Walbrook.

NACC. (n.d.). *Bush Food*. www.nacc.com.au/wp-content/uploads/2018/06/ Sharing-Noongar-Knowledge-Part-4-Bush-Foods.pdf

Natural Cancer Treatment. (2012). *Scaevola Spinescens – A traditional 'Bush Medicine'*. www.naturalcancertreatment.org/content/view/13/31

Natural Medicinal Herbs. (2017). www.naturalmedicinalherbs.net

Naughtin, K. (2018). Sharing Yamaji Knowledge. www.nacc.com.au/ wp-content/uploads/2018/06/Sharing-Yamaji-Knowledge-Education-Resource-low-res.pdf

Nevill, S. (2008). *Guide to the Wildflowers of Western Australia*. Perth: Simon Nevill Publications

New South Wales Flora Online. (2018). www.plantnet.rbgsyd.nsw.gov.au

Noongar Boodjar Language Centre. (2014). *Noongar Waangkiny: A learner's guide to Noongar* (2nd edn). Bachelor: Bachelor Press.

NQ Dry Tropics. (2015). *Dodder Laurel*. www.wiki.bdtnrm.org.au/index.php/ Dodder_Laurel

Nyalar Mirungan-ah Nature Refuge. (2013) *Plants Used by Aboriginal People*. www.cicadawoman.weebly.com/uploads/8/7/3/4/8734418/plants_used_by_aboriginal_people_april_2013.pdf

Nyungar Wardan Katitjin Bidi – Derbal Nara. (n.d.). *Wangkiny / Language Glossary*. www.derbalnara.org.au/wangkiny-language-glossary

Orchids of South-west Australia. (2018). *Caladenia – Spider Orchids*. www.chookman.id.au/wp_orchids/?page_id=1561

Outback Pride. (2015). *Passion Berry*. www.outbackpride.com.au/species/passion-berry

Oz Native Plants. (2018*).* www.oznativeplants.com

Oz Watergardens. (2018). *Edible Aquatic Plants*. www.ozwatergardens.com.au/

Pacific Bulb society. (2012). *Chamaescilla*. www.pacificbulbsociety.org/pbswiki/index.php/Chamaescilla

Palm and Cycad Societies of Australia. (2013). *Macrozamia fraseri*. www.pacsoa.org.au/wiki/Macrozamia_fraseri

Parks and Wildlife Service. (2018). *Milyu Nature Reserve*. www.parks.dpaw.wa.gov.au/site/milyu-nature-reserve

Pascoe, B. (2014). *Dark Emu Black Seeds: Agriculture of Accident?* Broome: Malaga Books Aboriginal Corporation.

Pereira, L. (2016). *Edible Seaweeds of the World*. London: CRC Press.

Perth NRM. (2016). *Traditional Ecological Knowledge of Forrestdale Lake*. www.perthnrm.com/wp-content/uploads/2016/09/Forrestdale-Lake-Traditional-Ecological-Database-WEB.pdf

Plants of the World Online. (2018). www.powo.science.kew.org

Perth Region NRM. (2015). *Traditional Ecological Knowledge*. www.perthnrm.com/wp-content/uploads/2016/09/Traditonal-Ecological-Knowledge-By-Noongar-Names-Jan-2016.pdf

Perth Region NRM. (n.d.a). *Noongar Words for Animals*. www.perthregionnrm.com/media/83493/noongar-words-for-animals-teacher-sheet.pdf

Perth Region NRM. (n.d.b) *Traditional Noongar Knowledge of Endangered Flora*. www.perthregionnrm.com/media/67417/tek-database-combined-document.pdf

Perth Region NRM. (n.d.c). *Traditional Ecological Knowledge of Forrestdale Lake*. www.perthregionnrm.com/media/91050/Forrestdale-Lake-Traditional-Ecological-Database-WEB.pdf

Perth Seed. (2010). *Persoonia longifolia - Snottygobble.* www.perthseed.com/persoonia-longifolia-snottygobble-p-411.html?osC-sid=744dddb44b6d3f2df3e59b346289800a

Peile, A. (1997). *Body and Soul: An Aboriginal View.* Perth: Hesperian Press.

Phillips, G. (2003). Life was not a walkabout for Victoria's Aborigines. *The Age,* 13 March.

PlantNET. (2018). www.plantnet.rbgsyd.nsw.gov.au/

Plants for a future. (2012). *Muehlenbeckia adpressa - (Labill.) Meissn.* www.pfaf.org/user/Plant.aspx?LatinName=Muehlenbeckia+adpressa

Rainbow Coast. (2017). *Noongar Seasons of the South Coast of Western Australia.* www.rainbowcoast.com.au/areas/rainbowcoast/seasons.htm

Rankmore, T. (2013). *Bush Medicine Plants of the Illawarra.* Wollongong, NSW: Illawarra Aboriginal Corporation.

Readford, H. (2011). *Pisolithus sp.* www.bushcraftoz.com/forums/showthread.php?7264-Pisolithus-sp&s=d2b0b887fc7c3de0cf9befa595d28fb3

Rippey, E. and B. Rowland. (2004). *Plants of the Perth Coast and Islands.* Perth: University of Western Australia Press.

Robinson, R. (2007a). *Fungus Fact Sheet 9.* www.dpaw.wa.gov.au/images/documents/about/science/fungus/9_2007-03_Pisolithus_albus_DEC_FF.pdf

Robinson, R. (2007b). *Laccocephalum mylittae – native bread.* www.dpaw.wa.gov.au/images/18_2007-12_Laccocephalum_mylittae_DEC_FF.pdf

Rogers Mushrooms. (2016). www.rogersmushrooms.com

Roleybushcare. (2015). *Snottygobble or Persoonia.* www.roleybushcare.com.au/bush-topics/119-snotty-gobble

Royal Botanic Gardens and Domain Trust. (n.d.). *Pteridium esculentum.* www.rbgsyd.nsw.gov.au/education/Resources/bush_foods/Pteridium_esculentum

Royal Botanic Gardens Victoria. (2015). *Pauridia vaginata.* www.data.rbg.vic.gov.au/vicflora/flora/taxon/bda6d15f-3d26-471c-880d-a96150611e13

Seeds of South Australia. (2017). *Chenopodium curvispicatum (Chenopodiaceae) White Goosefoot.* www.saseedbank.com.au/species_information.php?rid=1088

Shoebridge, B. (2004). *Edible Plants.* www.anpsa.org.au/APOL35/sep04-2.html

South East Regional Centre for Urban Land Care (SERCUL). (2014). *Bush Tucker Plant Fact Sheets.* www.SERCUL.org.au/bushtucker/BushTuckerPlantFactSheets.pdf

South East Regional Centre for Urban Land Care (SERCUL). (2014). *Coastal Pigface*. www.sercul.org.au/bushtucker/BushTuckerFactSheet_Pigface.pdf

South West Aboriginal Land & Sea Council (2016). *Kaartdijin Noongar – Noongar Knowledge – Food*. www.noongarculture.org.au/food/

State Flora. (2013). *South Australia's Native Coastal Flax Lily*. www.stateflora.sa.gov.au/about-us/latest-articles/native-flax-lily

Survival, Tracking and Awareness. (2012). *Typha*. www.survival.org.au/bf_typha.php.

Sustainable Gardening Australia. (2018). www.sgaonline.org.au

Taggart, A. (n.d.). *Local Edible Plants*. Australian Plants Society (Central Coast). Unpublished Paper.

Terra Perma Design. (2013). *Edible Weeds and Foraging in Perth*. www.terraperma.com.au/uploads/1/9/1/3/19138605/terra_perma_edible_weeds_workshop_booklet_v2_22-11-13.pdf

Terrestrial Orchids of South-West Australia. (2014). *Gastrodia lacista – Bell Orchid*. www.orchids.chookman.id.au/gastrodia/gastrodia.html

Tindale, N. (1974). *Aboriginal Tribes of Australia*. Canberra: Australian National University.

Tucker Bush. (2017). *WA Samphire – Tecticornia lepidosperma*. www.tuckerbush.com.au/wa-samphire-tecticornia-lepidosperma/

Useful Tropical Plants. (n.d.). *Tecticornia verrucosa*. www.tropical.theferns.info/viewtropical.php?id=Tecticornia+verrucosa

VicFlora. (2018). *Flora of Victoria*. www.vicflora.rbg.vic.gov.au

Victorian Resources Online. (2015). *Inland Pigface*. www.vro.agriculture.vic.gov.au/dpi/vro/vrosite.nsf/pages/water_sss_inland_pigface

Wahlquist, C. (2016). Evidence of 9,000-year-old stone houses found on Australian island. *The Guardian*. 5 September.

Watkinson, T. (n.d.). *Thelmitra (Sun Orchids)*. www.members.iinet.net.au/~emntee/Thelymitras%20Page%202.htm

Weeds of Australia. (2011). *Bluebell creeper – Billardiera fusiformis*. www.keyserver.lucidcentral.org/weeds/data/03030800-0b07-490a-8d04-0605030c0f01/media/Html/Billardiera_fusiformis.htm

Welsh, D. (2017) *Traditional Aboriginal Bush Foods*. www.aboriginalculture.com.au/bush_foods.html.

Western Australia's Wildflower Country. (2018). What's That Wildflower? www.wildflowercountry.com.au/wildflowers/whats-that-wildflower/

Wheatbelt Natural Resource Management (NRM). (n.d.). *The Badjaling Storybook.* www.wheatbeltnrm.org.au/sites/default/files/knowledge_hub/documents/badgaling_storybook_web.pdf

Wheatbelt Natural Resource Management (NRM). (2009) *Nyungar Budjara Wangany: Nyungar NRM Wordlist and Language Collection Booklet of the Avon Catchment Region.* www.wheatbeltnrm.org.au/sites/default/files/knowledge_hub/documents/nyungar-dictionary.pdf

Wheatbelt Natural Resource Management (NRM). (2015). *Boodjin: The Boyagin Rock Storybook.* www.wheatbeltnrm.org.au/sites/default/files/knowledge_hub/documents/Boodjin%20storybook%20-%20Web2.pdf

Wheatbelt Natural Resource Management (NRM). (2016). *Final Report: Tarin and North Tarin Rock BioBlitz.* http://wheatbeltnrm.org.au/sites/default/files/projects/files/Tarin%20and%20North%20Tarin%20Rock%20BioBlitz%20-%20Final%20Draft.pdf

Whitehurst, R. (1997). *Noongar Dictionary.* East Perth: Noongar Language and Culture Centre.

World Wide Wattle. (2013). www.worldwidewattle.com

Yelakitj Moort Nyungar Association Inc. (2008). *Bushtucker/Medicine.* www.Noongar.com.au/bushtucker.html.

Wild Magazine (n.d.) 10 Aboriginal Medicine Plants and Their Uses. Issue 151. www.wild.com.au.

Wildflower Society of WA. (n.d.). *Northern Suburbs Branch: Plant List.* www.ns.wsowa.org.au/plantlist

Williams, E. (1984). *Documentation and Archaeological Investigation of an Aboriginal Village Site in South Western Victoria.* www.nationalunitygovernment.org/pdf/Brough-Smythe-Papers-1840.pdf

Williams, A. and T. Sides. (2008). *Wiradjuri Plant Use in the Murrumbidgee Catchment.* www.archive.lls.nsw.gov.au/__data/assets/pdf_file/0009/495261/archive-wiradjuri-plant-use.pdf

Woodall, G., M. Moule, P. Eckersley, B. Boxshall and B. Puglisi. (2009). *Final Report to the Australian Flora Foundation on the project Cultivation of Native Potatoes (Platysace spp.).* www.aff.org.au/Woodall_native_potato_final.pdf

Yarra Ranges. (2009). *Wahlenbergia communis.* fe.yarraranges.vic.gov.au/Residents/Trees_Vegetation/Yarra_Ranges_Plant_Directory/Yarra_Ranges_Local_Plant_Directory/Lower_Storey/Herbs_and_Groundcovers_1m/Wahlenbergia_communis

Yarra Ranges. (2010a). *Wahlenbergia gracilenta*. fe.yarraranges.vic.gov.au/
Residents/Trees_Vegetation/Yarra_Ranges_Plant_Directory/Yarra_Ranges_
Local_Plant_Directory/Lower_Storey/Herbs_and_Groundcovers_1m/
Wahlenbergia_gracilenta

Yarra Ranges. (2010b). *Schoenoplectus tabernaemontani*. fe.yarraranges.vic.
gov.au/Residents/Trees_Vegetation/Yarra_Ranges_Plant_Directory/Yarra_
Ranges_Local_Plant_Directory/Lower_Storey/Aquatic_and_Semi-aquatic/
Schoenoplectus_tabernaemontani

Image credits

p. 225   Salt Paperbark, photo by Geoff Derrin

p. 226   Banbar, photo by Jean Hort

Broom Bush, photo by John Fleming

p. 227   Chenille Honeymyrtle, photo by Geoff Derrin

p. 228   Midget Greenhood Orchid, photo by Reiner Richter

p. 229   Midget Greenhood Orchid, photo by Tristan Kennedy

p. 230   Milkmaids, photo by Bill and Mark Bell

p. 231   Milkmaids, photo by Bill and Mark Bell

p. 232   Nardoo, photo by Mark Marathon

p. 233   Nardoo, photo by Mark Marathon

p. 234   Native Bluebell, photo by Harry Rose

p. 235   Native Bluebell, photo by Ian Fraser

p. 237   Native Cranberry, photo by Marion Cambridge

p. 239   Native Geranium, photo by Harry Rose

p. 240   Native Hibiscus, photographer unknown

p. 241   Native Hibiscus, photographer unknown

p. 242   Native Myrtle, photo by Mark Marathon

p. 243   Native Myrtle, photo by Mark Marathon

p. 244   Native Plantain, photo by Russell Cumming

p. 245   Native Plantain, photo by Russell Cumming

p. 246   Native Poplar, photo by Steven and Allison Pearson

p. 247   Native Poplar, photo by Mark Marathon

p. 248   Native Spinach, photo by Anna (photo in public domain)

p. 249   Native Spinach, photo by Eugene Arbeit

p. 251   Neptune's Necklace, photo by Andrea Schaffer

p. 252   Nitre Bush, photo by William Archer

p. 253   Nitre Bush, photo by William Archer

p. 254   Nodding Chocolate Lily, photo by Jean Hort

p. 255   Nodding Chocolate Lily, photographer unknown

p. 256   Old Man Saltbush, photo by John Horsfall

p. 257   Old Man Saltbush, photo by John Horsfall

p. 258   One-sided Bottlebrush, photo by William Archer

p. 259   One-sided Bottlebrush, photo by William Archer

p. 260   Oondoroo, photo by R. Hotchkiss

p. 261   Oondoroo, photo by Stephen L. (photo in public domain)

p. 262   Pale Grass-lily, photo by Harry Rose

p. 263   Pale Grass-lily, photo by Russell Cumming

p. 264   Pale Rush, photo by Clare Snow

p. 265   Pale Rush, photo by Daderot

p. 266   Parakeelya, photo by kirinaliza

p. 267   Parakeelya, photo by Russell Cumming

p. 268   Passion Berry, photo by M. Fagg

p. 269   Passion Berry, photo by Russell Cumming

p. 270   Pincushion Mistletoe, photo by Roger Fryer and Jill Newland

p. 271   Pincushion Mistletoe, photo by Roger Fryer and Jill Newland

Index

www.ingramcontent.com/pod-product-compliance
Lightning Source LLC
Chambersburg PA
CBHW050803270326
41926CB00025B/4513